Keynote 1

David Bohlke

NATIONAL GEOGRAPHIC LEARNING | CENGAGE Learning·

Australia • Brazil • Mexico • Singapore • United Kingdom • United States

NATIONAL GEOGRAPHIC LEARNING | **CENGAGE Learning**

Keynote 1
David Bohlke

Publisher: Andrew Robinson

Executive Editor: Sean Bermingham

Senior Development Editor: Derek Mackrell

Development Editor: Christopher Street

Director of Global Marketing: Ian Martin

Senior Product Marketing Manager:
Caitlin Thomas

IP Analyst: Kyle Cooper

IP Project Manager: Carissa Poweleit

Media Researcher: Leila Hishmeh

Senior Director of Production: Michael Burggren

Senior Content Project Manager: Tan Jin Hock

Manufacturing Planner: Mary Beth Hennebury

Compositor: SPi Global

Cover/Text Design: Brenda Carmichael

Cover Photo: A bird's eye view of the High Line,
New York: © Diane Cook and Len Jenshel/
National Geographic Creative

For product information and technology assistance, contact us at
Cengage Learning Customer & Sales Support, 1-800-354-9706

For permission to use material from this text or product,
submit all requests online at **cengage.com/permissions**
Further permissions questions can be emailed to
permissionrequest@cengage.com

Student Book with My Keynote Online:
ISBN-13: 978-1-337-10410-4

Student Book:
ISBN-13: 978-1-305-96503-4

National Geographic Learning
20 Channel Center Street
Boston, MA 02210
USA

Cengage Learning is a leading provider of customized learning solutions with office locations around the globe, including Singapore, the United Kingdom, Australia, Mexico, Brazil, and Japan.

Visit National Geographic Learning online at **NGL.cengage.com**
Visit our corporate website at **www.cengage.com**

Printed in China
Print Number: 07   Print Year: 2020

Contents

Featured **TED**TALKS

Sleepy Man Banjo Boys

1 Bluegrass from New Jersey

Jessi Arrington

2 Wearing nothing new

Chris Burkard

3 The joy of surfing in ice-cold water

Tom Thum

4 The orchestra in my mouth

Yves Rossy

5 Fly with the Jetman

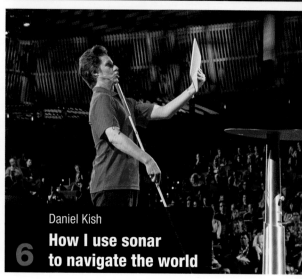

Daniel Kish

6 How I use sonar to navigate the world

Scope and Sequence

UNIT		VOCABULARY	LISTENING	LANGUAGE FOCUS	SPEAKING
		LESSON A		**LESSON B**	
1 Passions		Music and movie genres	**My passion for music** *Phillip Jones, musician*	**Function** Talking about likes and interests **Grammar** Simple present	I like hip-hop a lot
2 Spending Habits		Things we spend money on	**How I spend my money** *Stella Hekker, student*	**Function** Talking about habits and routines **Grammar** Simple present with adverbs of frequency	Take a guess
3 Career Paths		Job titles	**Interview with a TV presenter** *Richard Lenton, journalist*	**Function** Asking about and describing jobs **Grammar** *like* vs. *would like*	A future job

PRESENTATION 1   Introducing someone you know

UNIT		VOCABULARY	LISTENING	LANGUAGE FOCUS	SPEAKING
4 Talents		Collocations to describe abilities	**A unique ability** *Okotanpe, contact juggler*	**Function** Describing abilities and talents **Grammar** *can/can't*	A talented class
5 Technology		Adjectives to describe gadgets	**How I used drones to make an amazing video** *Sam Cossman, explorer*	**Function** Describing things and how they work **Grammar** Quantifiers	Wearable technology
6 Challenges		Daily challenges	**It's no big deal** *Vasu Sojitra, skier*	**Function** Describing sequence **Grammar** Time clauses	Dealing with exam stress

PRESENTATION 2   Presenting a favorite piece of technology

LESSON C	LESSON D		LESSON E	
READING	**TED TALK**	**PRESENTATION SKILLS**	**COMMUNICATE**	**WRITING**
Bluegrass for a new generation	**BLUEGRASS FROM NEW JERSEY** *Sleepy Man Banjo Boys*	Introducing yourself	Getting to know you	Write an email to introduce yourself
Buy nothing new	**WEARING NOTHING NEW** *Jessi Arrington*	Using effective body language	Are you a green shopper?	Writing a social media post
A dancer's dream	**THE JOY OF SURFING IN ICE-COLD WATER** *Chris Burkard*	Thanking the audience	What's my job?	Writing about a dream job
Pro gaming: A dream career?	**THE ORCHESTRA IN MY MOUTH** *Tom Thum*	Introducing a topic	Recommending a job	Writing about someone with an unusual ability
Flying like a bird	**FLY WITH THE JETMAN** *Yves Rossy*	Using gestures effectively	A new app	Writing a review of a piece of technology
Living without fear	**HOW I USE SONAR TO NAVIGATE THE WORLD** *Daniel Kish*	Involving your audience	Dos and don'ts	Writing about a person who overcame a challenge

Scope and Sequence

UNIT		VOCABULARY	LISTENING	LANGUAGE FOCUS	SPEAKING
				LESSON A → **LESSON B**	
7 Confidence		Adjectives for describing appearance and personality	**Like mother, like daughter** *Bonnie Kim, school consultant*	**Function** Describing people **Grammar** Modifying adverbs	A movie of your life
8 Wild Places		Natural places	**An amazing place** *Ross Donihue and Marty Schnure, cartographers*	**Function** Making comparisons **Grammar** Comparative and superlative adjectives	What do you know?
9 Achievements		Collocations for describing personal achievements	**My great achievement** *Scott Leefe, marathon runner*	**Function** Talking about the past **Grammar** Simple past	Round-the-world adventure

PRESENTATION 3   Describing an amazing place you visited

UNIT		VOCABULARY	LISTENING	LANGUAGE FOCUS	SPEAKING
10 Creative Cities		Collocations for describing neighborhoods	**The neighborhood where I grew up** *Craig Albrightson, lecturer*	**Function** Offering suggestions **Grammar** *should/shouldn't*	The right neighborhood
11 Picture Perfect		Nouns and adjectives related to photography	**My perfect photo** *Hannah Reyes, photographer*	**Function** Asking for and giving opinions **Grammar** Sense verbs	Is it real?
12 Healthy Habits		Collocations for talking about good and bad habits	**My healthy (and unhealthy) habits** *David Matijasevich, teacher*	**Function** Talking about real conditions **Grammar** Real conditionals	Healthy choices

PRESENTATION 4   Describing an issue or challenge in your community

| LESSON C | LESSON D | | LESSON E | |
READING	TED TALK	PRESENTATION SKILLS	COMMUNICATE	WRITING
Pressure to be "perfect"	**WHY THINKING YOU'RE UGLY IS BAD FOR YOU** *Meaghan Ramsey*	Adding support by giving statistics	A class poll	Writing about a friend
An otherworldly place	**UNSEEN FOOTAGE, UNTAMED NATURE** *Karen Bass*	Showing enthusiasm	A tourism poster	Writing about a place you'd like to visit
Extreme survival	**LET'S SAVE THE LAST PRISTINE CONTINENT** *Robert Swan*	Pausing effectively	An achievement	Writing about someone who achieved something
Reshaping a city	**HOW TO REVIVE A NEIGHBORHOOD** *Theaster Gates*	Paraphrasing key points	Planning neighborhood improvements	Write suggestions for improving your town
Unreal images of nature	**IMPOSSIBLE PHOTOGRAPHY** *Erik Johansson*	Introducing a visual	Animal hybrids	Writing about a photograph
A simple solution	**THE SIMPLE POWER OF HANDWASHING** *Myriam Sidibe*	Getting the audience's attention	Fact or myth?	Writing health tips

Welcome to Keynote!

In this book, you will develop your English language skills and explore great ideas with an authentic TED Talk. Each unit topic is based around a TED speaker's main idea.

In Unit 10, Theaster Gates shares his ideas for building creative neighborhoods that connect and inspire the people who live there.

LISTENING AND SPEAKING

- Practice listening to real people talking about the unit topic. Real-life people featured in this book include a musician, a journalist, and an explorer.

- Develop your **speaking confidence** with a model conversation and guided speaking tasks.

See pages 111, 113

VOCABULARY AND GRAMMAR

- In each unit, you'll learn key words, phrases, and grammar structures for talking about the unit topic.

- Build **language and visual literacy skills** with real-life information—in Unit 10, you'll discover eight keys for making a great neighborhood.

See pages 110, 112

READING

- Develop your **reading and vocabulary skills** with a specially adapted reading passage. In Unit 10, you'll learn how an artist is reshaping an entire neighborhood.

- The passage includes several words and phrases that appear later in the TED Talk.

See pages 114–115

VIEWING

- Practice your viewing and **critical thinking** skills as you watch a specially adapted TED Talk.

- Notice how TED speakers use effective language and **communication** skills to present their ideas.

See pages 116–117

COMMUNICATING AND PRESENTING

- Use your **creativity** and **collaboration skills** in a final task that reviews language and ideas from the unit.

See page 118

- Build your **speaking confidence** further in a Presentation task (after every three units).

See page 139

WRITING

- Communicate your own ideas about the unit topic in a controlled writing task.

See page 118

- Develop your **writing and language skills** further in the **Keynote Workbook** and online at **MyKeynoteOnline**.

What is **TED** ?

TED has a simple goal: to spread great ideas. Every year, hundreds of presenters share ideas at TED events around the world. Millions of people watch TED Talks online. The talks inspire many people to change their attitudes and their lives.

SPREADING IDEAS WORLDWIDE

Over **10,000**
TEDx events in
167 countries

Over **2,200**
TEDTALKS recorded

TEDTALKS
translated into
105 languages

Over
1,000,000,000
views of **TED**TALKS at TED.com

1 Passions

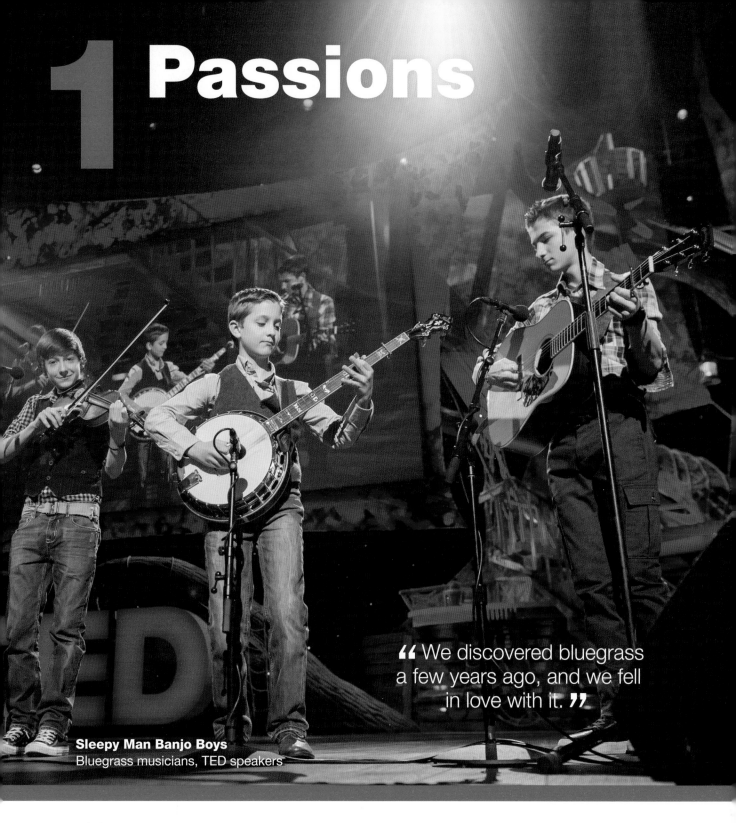

“ We discovered bluegrass a few years ago, and we fell in love with it. **”**

Sleepy Man Banjo Boys
Bluegrass musicians, TED speakers

UNIT GOALS

In this unit, you will …

• talk about likes and interests.

• read about three young musicians.

• watch a TED Talk about the joy of performing music.

WARM UP

▶ **1.1** Watch part of Sleepy Man Banjo Boys' TED Talk. Answer the questions with a partner.

1 Do you like the boys' music? Why or why not?

2 Who's your favorite musician?

A musician plays the banjo outside his house.

1A Do you like country music?

VOCABULARY Likes

A Complete the chart below using the words in the box.

action	✓classical	✓country / folk	horror
✓jazz	✓rock	romantic comedy	science fiction

Types of music	Types of movies
Jazz	
Classical	
Rock	

B Work with a partner. Add two more words to each column.

C Work with a partner. What types of music and movies do you like?

> I like romantic comedies.
> How about you?

> I like action movies.

14

LISTENING My passion for music

Previewing a task
Before you listen, look carefully at the task. Read all the words and ask yourself, "What am I listening for?" Think about possible words you may hear.

A ▶ **1.2** Philip Jones is a musician. Watch and check [✓] the musical instruments he owns.

- ☐ bass guitar
- ☐ banjo
- ☐ acoustic guitar
- ☐ mandolin
- ☐ ukulele
- ☐ electric guitar

B ▶ **1.2** Watch again. Complete the sentences.

1 "I love listening to music, but I also like _____ and recording my own songs."

2 "I'm a member of an Irish _____ band."

C CRITICAL THINKING

Personalizing Do you like the music that Philip Jones's band plays? Discuss with a partner.

Philip Jones performs live.

SPEAKING Talking about favorites

A ▶ **1.3** Do the two people like the same kind of music?

A: Oh, listen! This is my favorite piece of music!

B: Really? Who's the composer?

A: Bach. I love his music.   like his music a lot / really like his music

B: Yeah? I don't know him very well.

A: Oh, I think his music is amazing.   incredible / wonderful

B: Yeah? I don't like classical music so much.   that much / very much

A: Really? So what kind of music do you like?   sort of / type of

B: Anything really. My favorite singer is Bruno Mars.

B Practice the conversation with a partner. Practice again using the words on the right.

C Write one favorite for each category. Work in a group. Share your ideas.

1 singer: _____

2 song: _____

3 actor: _____

4 movie: _____

My favorite singer is Taylor Swift.

Really? What's your favorite song?

1B What's your favorite?

LANGUAGE FOCUS Discussing favorites

A ▶ **1.4** Read the information below. Which age group likes each type of music the most?

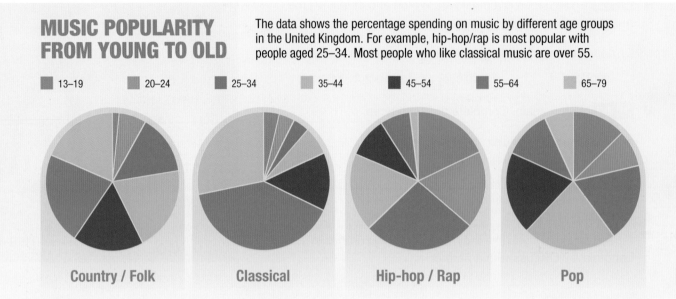

MUSIC POPULARITY FROM YOUNG TO OLD

The data shows the percentage spending on music by different age groups in the United Kingdom. For example, hip-hop/rap is most popular with people aged 25–34. Most people who like classical music are over 55.

■ 13–19   ■ 20–24   ■ 25–34   ■ 35–44   ■ 45–54   ■ 55–64   ■ 65–79

Country / Folk   Classical   Hip-hop / Rap   Pop

B ▶ **1.5** Two people are talking about the information above. Watch and circle the correct words.

1 The man's grandmother (**likes**/**doesn't like**) classical music. She (**likes**/**doesn't like**) pop music.

2 The man (**likes**/**doesn't like**) rap music. He (**loves**/**hates**) pop music.

C ▶ **1.6** Watch and study the language in the chart.

Talking about likes and interests			
What's your favorite movie?	My favorite movie is *Transformers*.		
Who are your favorite actors?	My favorite actors are Matt Damon and Will Smith.		
Do you like K-pop? Does he like R&B?	Yes, I do. / No, I don't. I like country music. Yes, he does. / No, he doesn't. He likes jazz.		
What kind of music do you like?	I	love really like	hip-hop.
		like hip-hop	a lot.
What kind of music don't you like?	I	don't like	pop	at all. very much.
		hate	pop.	

For more information on **simple present**, see Grammar Summary 1 on page 155.

D Match each question to the best response.

1 What's your favorite movie?　　　　○　　　○ No, she doesn't. 5

2 Do you like action movies?　　　　○　　　○ I hate classical music. 4

3 Who are your favorite singers?　　○　　　○ *The Martian*. 1

4 What kind of music don't you like?　○　　　○ I like science fiction movies. 6

5 Does your teacher like country music?　○　○ Yes, I do. 2

6 What kind of movies do you like?　　○　　　○ Nicki Minaj and Rihanna. 3

E Work with a partner. Answer the questions in **D** with your own information.

F ▶ **1.7** Complete the information. Circle the correct words. Listen and check your answers.

Tyler Spencer lives in Oregon, in the United States. He has an unusual hobby. He ¹(**like**/**likes**) to play the didgeridoo, a traditional instrument from Australia.

Tyler doesn't really ²(**like**/**likes**) to buy didgeridoos. He prefers to make his own. His favorite materials to work with ³(**is**/**are**) bamboo, oak, and other hardwoods.

These days more and more people ⁴(**like**/**likes**) to play the didgeridoo. Oregon's InDidjInUs festival attracts visitors from around the world. Tyler likes the festival ⁵(**at all**/**very much**) because he can meet people who share his passion.

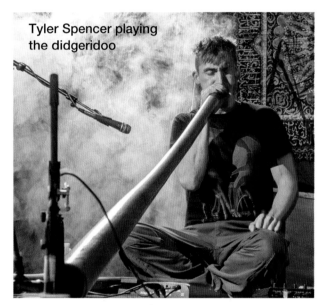

Tyler Spencer playing the didgeridoo

SPEAKING I like hip-hop a lot.

A Write two things you like and one thing you don't like for each category.

Types of music	Singer or group	Types of movies

B Listen to your partner's three things. Guess which one your partner doesn't like.

I'll go first: K-pop, rock, and hip-hop.

I think you like K-pop and hip-hop. You don't like rock.

You're wrong. I don't like K-pop at all. I love rock.

1C Bluegrass for a new generation

Sleepy Man Banjo Boys: Robbie, Tommy, and Jonny Mizzone

PRE-READING Skimming

A Skim the reading. How did the boys become interested in bluegrass?

a They saw a music video online.

b Their music teacher loved bluegrass.

c They went to a bluegrass concert.

B Read the passage. Check your answer to **A**.

▶ 1.8

Not many teenagers would say that they really like folk music. But Sleepy Man Banjo Boys are different—their passion is bluegrass,[1] and they're bringing it to a new generation.[2]

The **band** is made up of three teenage brothers from New Jersey, United States—a place which is known more for its rock music. So how did they start playing bluegrass?

The boys were on YouTube one day and saw an old music video of Earl Scruggs—a famous bluegrass musician. "We were like, 'Wow, we've never heard anything like this,'" says Tommy. The boys listened to some more songs, started learning some **traditional** bluegrass music, and the band was born.

A short time later, they posted a YouTube video of themselves playing music at home. People were **amazed** to see such young boys playing bluegrass so well. Millions of people watched the video, and just two weeks later, the boys appeared on TV for the first time.

The brothers are now starting to **create** their own kind of bluegrass music, writing their own songs and adding lyrics.[3] "We're not singing about, you know, the old country road and the barn,"[4] explains Tommy. "I'm not saying that's bad, but we're singing about more **modern** things."

---

[1] **bluegrass:** *n.* a type of folk music that started in the United States
[2] **generation:** *n.* a group of people of a similar age

[3] **lyrics:** *n.* the words to a song
[4] **barn:** *n.* a building on a farm to keep animals in

UNDERSTANDING MAIN IDEAS

Which of the following does the passage mention?

☐ where the boys are from

☐ how the boys became famous

☐ the boys' favorite song

☐ the type of things the boys sing about

UNDERSTANDING DETAILS

Circle **T** for true or **F** for false.

1 The three boys in the band are related to each other.   **T**   **F**

2 Sleepy Man Banjo Boys started as a rock band.   **T**   **F**

3 New Jersey is famous for bluegrass music.   **T**   **F**

4 The band's first YouTube video showed them on TV.   **T**   **F**

5 Sleepy Man Banjo Boys make their own bluegrass songs.   **T**   **F**

UNDERSTANDING SEQUENCE

Number the events (1–6) in the order they happened.

a __3__ The brothers make a video and put it on YouTube.

b __2__ The brothers start to learn some bluegrass songs.

c __6__ The brothers appear on TV.

d __4__ Many people watch the video.

e __5__ The brothers start to write their own bluegrass songs.

f __1__ The brothers watch a YouTube video of a famous bluegrass musician.

BUILDING VOCABULARY

A Choose the correct option to complete the sentences.

1 An example of a **band** is _____.

  a Earl Scruggs   **b** Sleepy Man Banjo Boys

2 An example of a **modern** instrument is _____.

  a an electric guitar   **b** a banjo

3 An example of a **traditional** type of music is _____.

  a country   **b** rap

4 If you **create** something, you _____ it.

  a find   **b** make

5 If you are **amazed**, you are very _____.

  a happy   **b** surprised

B CRITICAL THINKING

Personalizing What kinds of **traditional** music come from your country? What are the **traditional** instruments?

1D Bluegrass from New Jersey

TEDTALKS

SLEEPY MAN BANJO BOYS are from the U.S. **state** of New Jersey—what they jokingly call "the bluegrass **capital** of the **world**." These young brothers were inspired to teach themselves a new kind of music and share it with the world. Their idea worth spreading is that making music brings equal **joy** to the musicians and the listeners.

PREVIEWING

Read the paragraph above. Match each **bold** word to its meaning. You will hear these words in the TED Talk.

1 planet Earth: _____

2 happiness: _JOY_____

3 main place for an activity: _____

4 a region of a country: _state._____

VIEWING

A ▶ **1.9** Watch the TED Talk. Match each name to the correct age and instrument.

1 10   **Tommy**   fiddle

2 14   **Jonny**   banjo

3 15   **Robbie**   guitar

B Look at the picture on page 21. Tell your partner about each person.

> This is Tommy. He's 15, and he plays guitar.

C ▶ **1.9** Watch the TED Talk again. How did the band get its name?

  a When Jonny started to play the banjo, he was very little and often fell asleep.

  b When the boys first started playing bluegrass, the music made them feel sleepy.

  c When Jonny first started to play the banjo, it looked like he was sleeping.

D CRITICAL THINKING

Inference   Why does the audience laugh after Tommy says, "We're three brothers from New Jersey—you know, the bluegrass capital of the world"?

  a It's unusual for brothers to play bluegrass.

  b New Jersey is not at all famous for bluegrass.

  c Bluegrass is popular in the United States but not the rest of the world.

VOCABULARY IN CONTEXT

▶ **1.10** Watch the excerpts from the TED Talk. Choose the correct meaning of the words.

PRESENTATION SKILLS Introducing yourself

> When you present, it's sometimes a good idea to introduce yourself. You can give your name and some additional information about your interest in the topic. You can introduce yourself informally or formally.
>
> **Informally**
> I'm ...
>
> **Formally**
> I'd like to introduce myself. My name is ...

A ▶ **1.11** Watch Robbie introduce the band. Complete the sentence.

"I'm just going to take a second to _____."

B ▶ **1.11** Watch again. After he gives his name, what other information does he include?

C Work in a group. Introduce yourself. Include your name and other information.

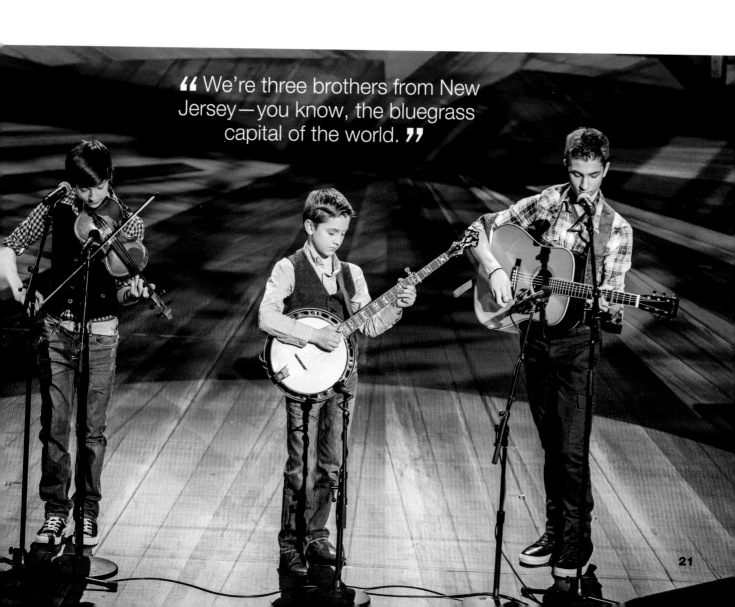

“ We're three brothers from New Jersey—you know, the bluegrass capital of the world. ”

1E Class favorites

COMMUNICATE Getting to know you

A Look at the chart below. Add one more category to the list.

Find someone who likes …	Name	Favorite
romantic comedies	Yes, she does	one day
songs in English	Yes,	show: show me.
video games	Yes	Sonic.
rap music	Yes NO	
foreign movies		later.
K-pop	NO	
horror movies		conjuro
_____	Yes	lop in.

B Walk around the classroom. Find someone who likes each thing. Write his or her name and then ask a follow-up question to find out his or her favorite.

C Work in a group. Share interesting or surprising information you heard.

> **Showing interest**
> *Really?   Yeah?   Wow!   Cool!   That's great!*

WRITING An email

A Complete the information about yourself.

Name: _____   Where from: _____   Age: _____

School year: _____   Your passion: _____

B Write an email to a classmate. Introduce yourself. Include information about your passion.

> Hi, Kara.
>
> My name's Teresa. I'm from Tutunendo, Colombia. I'm 19 years old and a first-year student at the University of Medellín. My passion in life is tennis. My favorite tennis player is Serena Williams. I also play tennis every weekend at my local club. I really love it. Write soon!
>
> Teresa

2 Spending Habits

" I'm outfit-obsessed. I love finding, wearing, and more recently, photographing and blogging a different, colorful, crazy outfit for every single occasion. But I don't buy anything new. "

Jessi Arrington
Designer, TED speaker

UNIT GOALS

In this unit, you will …

- talk about money and spending.
- read about the benefits of buying nothing new.
- watch a TED Talk about an unusual fashion style.

WARM UP

▶ **2.1** Watch part of Jessi Arrington's TED Talk. Answer the questions with a partner.

1 What do you think "outfit-obsessed" means?

2 Where do you think Jessi gets her clothes?

A woman shopping in the Old City Market, Jerusalem

2A What do you like to buy?

VOCABULARY Spending money

A Complete the word web below using the words in the box.

| bus pass | camera | coffee | concerts | haircuts | shirts ✓ |

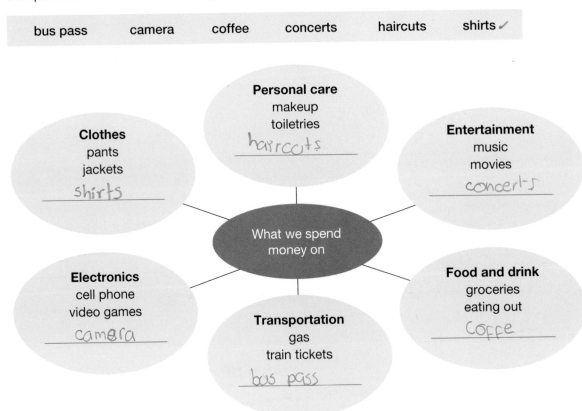

Clothes
pants
jackets
shirts

Personal care
makeup
toiletries
haircuts

Entertainment
music
movies
concerts

What we spend money on

Electronics
cell phone
video games
camera

Transportation
gas
train tickets
bus pass

Food and drink
groceries
eating out
coffe

B Work with a partner. Which of the things in the word web can you buy secondhand?

You can buy video games secondhand.

Right. And you can buy cameras secondhand, too.

LISTENING How I spend my money

> **Listening for negation**
> When listening, it's important to be able to identify negation.
> Speakers often use contractions such as:
> *don't/doesn't*   *isn't/aren't*   *can't*

A ▶ **2.2** Stella Hekker is a student. Watch and check [✓] the things that she spends a lot of money on.

☐ car   ☑ concerts
☑ eating out   ☐ clothes
☐ makeup   ☐ cell phone

Stella Hekker

B ▶ **2.2** Watch again. What does Stella say her friends spend a lot of money on? Why is Stella different? Discuss with a partner.

C **CRITICAL THINKING**

Comparing How are you and Stella similar? How are you different? Discuss with a partner.

SPEAKING Talking about shops

A ▶ **2.3** Where do the two people decide to go shopping?

A: Do you want to go shopping after class?

B: Sure. Where do you want to go?   OK / Yeah

A: Well, I usually go to Market Street. They have   often / sometimes
some great designer shops there.

B: Oh. Do you ever go to City Mall?

A: No, never. Why?   Hardly ever / Rarely

B: There's a great secondhand clothes store
there. I go every week.   once a week / twice a month

A: OK, good idea! To be honest, I need to
start saving more money.

B Practice the conversation with a partner. Practice again using the words on the right.

C Write the names of three places where you shop.

1 _____   **2** _____   **3** _____

Work with a partner. Ask each other about where you shop.

Where do you like to shop?

I sometimes shop at the mall.

Yeah? Why do you like it?

2B Do you ever shop online?

LANGUAGE FOCUS Discussing spending habits

A ▶ **2.4** Read the information. What do students in the United States spend most of their money on?

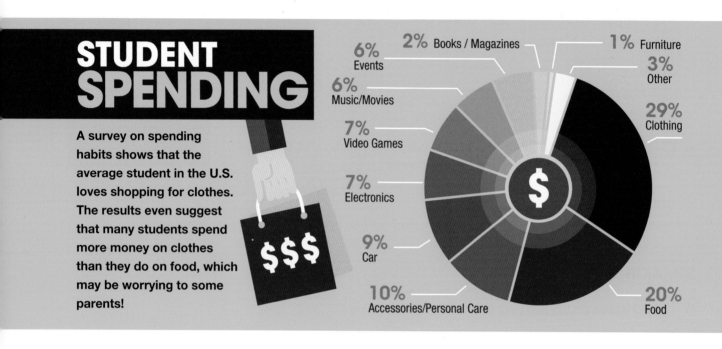

STUDENT SPENDING

A survey on spending habits shows that the average student in the U.S. loves shopping for clothes. The results even suggest that many students spend more money on clothes than they do on food, which may be worrying to some parents!

$$$

2% Books / Magazines
1% Furniture
6% Events
3% Other
6% Music/Movies
29% Clothing
7% Video Games
7% Electronics
9% Car
10% Accessories/Personal Care
20% Food

B ▶ **2.5** Two people are talking about spending habits. Watch and circle **T** for true or **F** for false.

1 The boy's spending habits are similar to those shown in the chart.   **T**   **F**

2 The girl's spending habits are similar to those shown in the chart.   **T**   **F**

C ▶ **2.6** Watch and study the language in the chart.

Talking about habits and routines			
Do you ever shop online?	Yes, I	always usually often sometimes	shop online.
Do you ever buy furniture?	No, I	hardly ever / rarely never	buy furniture.
How often do you go shopping?	I go shopping	every day. once / twice / three times a week.	
	I never go shopping.		

For more information on **adverbs of frequency** and **time expressions**, see Grammar Summary 2 on page 155.

26

D Unscramble the words to make questions.

1 ever / you / buy / do / magazines ? _Do you ever buy magazines?_

2 you / do / ever / online / shop ? _Do you ever shop online_

3 how / spend / you / do / often / money / on clothes ? _How often do you spend money on clothes_

4 often / how / you / buy / do / new / shoes ? _How often do you buy new shoes?_

E Work with a partner. Ask and answer the questions in **D**.

F ▶ **2.7** Complete the information. Circle the correct words. Listen and check your answers.

When shopping for new clothes, we ¹(**ever** /**usually**) think very carefully about the style, the color, and the price. But how ²(**often**/ **usually**) do you consider the environment?

ECOALF is a clothing company that is trying to help the environment. They make new clothes using recycled materials. They recycle things like old tires, plastic bottles, and ³(**hardly ever** /**sometimes**) fishing nets. They even use coffee grounds that they collect from different coffee shops ⁴(**once**/**every**) day.

OVER **40** MILLION PLASTIC BOTTLES RECYCLED SO FAR

because there is no planet B

ECOALF jackets made from recycled bottles

But ECOALF believes that style is important, too, so the clothes they make ⁵(**never** /**always**) look recycled. In this way, ECOALF hopes people realize that they can help the environment and look good at the same time.

SPEAKING Take a guess

A Work with a partner. How often do you think he or she buys these things? Write time phrases (e.g., *every day, twice a week, never*) in the *My guesses* column.

How often do you buy …?	My guesses	Partner's answers
shoes	harly ever	she boys somtimes
video games	never	never
books	sometimes	sometimes
coffee	I never buy coffee	harly ever
makeup	I sometime buy makeup	often
music	I never buy music	usual
furniture	I never buy muebles	lately

B Interview your partner and write the answers. How many guesses are correct?

How often do you buy shoes?

Let's see. … I buy shoes about once a month.

Shoppers at Hell's Kitchen flea market, New York

2c Buy nothing new

PRE-READING Previewing

Read the first paragraph of the passage. Do you think the challenge is easy or difficult? Discuss with a partner.

▶ 2.8

1   Could you live for one month without buying anything new? Buy Nothing New Month started in Australia in 2010. It challenges people once a year to buy nothing new—except

5 food, **products** used for hygiene,[1] and medicine— for 30 days.

  The aim is to encourage people to be less wasteful and to make us think about the impact[2] our shopping habits have on the **environment**.

10 But the challenge is not simply about going without.[3] People can find other, creative ways to get the things they want. Here are a few examples of how to buy nothing new.

Shopping secondhand

15 Many people shop for secondhand products at places like thrift stores and flea markets. You can usually find a wide variety of items at phenomenal[4] prices, and your money often goes to a good cause.[5] And while you're there, why not **donate** something

20 you no longer use so someone else can buy it?

Swapping

With the Internet, **swapping** is easier than ever before. There are many websites, such as swap.com, where you can post a photo of something you don't need.

25 Then, other users can offer something as a swap.

Upcycling

Upcycling involves turning something you no longer need into something much more useful. For example, you can turn an empty drink bottle into a beautiful

30 vase, or an old door into an interesting table.

  So why not try the challenge for yourself? You can be a friend to the environment and also to your **wallet**.

[1] **hygiene:** *n.* the practice of keeping yourself clean
[2] **impact:** *n.* effect
[3] **go without:** *phrasal verb* to not use or do something

[4] **phenomenal:** *adj.* unusually great
[5] **a good cause:** *phrase* something that helps other people, e.g., a charity

UNDERSTANDING MAIN IDEAS

A Read the passage. Check [✓] the aims of Buy Nothing New Month.

[✓] to help people realize that what they buy can affect the environment

[ ] to help people better understand what life is like for poor people

[ ] to help people think more carefully about throwing things away

B According to the passage, which of these items are OK to buy during Buy Nothing New Month?

[ ] a cup of coffee from a café

[✓] a bottle of shampoo

[ ] a new T-shirt for your friend's birthday

[ ] a new tie for a job interview

[ ] a computer game from your best friend

UNDERSTANDING EXAMPLES

A Find and <u>underline</u> examples of the following in the article.

1 three types of products you can buy during Buy Nothing New Month

2 two places where you can buy secondhand products 3

3 a website where you can swap items

4 two examples of upcycling

B Which of the following describes an example of upcycling?

a donating your old clothes to a secondhand shop

b fixing a broken table rather than throwing it away

c making a new scarf using old socks

BUILDING VOCABULARY

A Complete each sentence with a word from the box.

donate	environment	products	swap	wallet

1 Many people _donate_ things they don't need to charity shops.

2 It's OK to buy healthcare _products_ during Buy Nothing New Month.

3 Some people hold parties where they _swap_ clothes with their friends.

4 Throwing things away when they are still in good condition is bad for the _environment_ .

5 At the end of Buy Nothing New Month, you may have more money than usual in your _wallet_ .

B **CRITICAL THINKING**

Evaluating Do you think Buy Nothing New Month is a good way to help the **environment**? Discuss with a partner.

2D Wearing nothing new

TED TALKS

JESSI ARRINGTON loves to wear **crazy,** colorful **outfits**. But she never buys new clothes. Instead, she buys **unique** secondhand clothes for her **wardrobe**. Her idea worth spreading is that secondhand shopping can reduce our impact on the environment and our wallets, while still being fun and creative.

PREVIEWING

Read the paragraph above. Match each **bold** word to its meaning. You will hear these words in the TED Talk.

1 clothes worn together: _____

3 not ordinary: _____

2 one-of-a-kind: _____

4 all the clothes you own: _____

VIEWING

A ▶ **2.9** Watch Part 1 of the TED Talk. What three things does Arrington consider when she chooses her outfits? Discuss with a partner.

B Read the excerpts from the next part of Arrington's TED Talk. Which outfit below do you think each excerpt refers to? Discuss with a partner.

1 "So let's start with Sunday. I call this 'Shiny Tiger.'"

2 "Monday: Color is powerful."

3 "Friday: ... Gold sequins go with everything."

C ▶ **2.10** Watch Part 2 of the TED Talk. Check your guesses.

D CRITICAL THINKING

Reflecting Read the statements below from Arrington's TED Talk. Do you agree?
Discuss with a partner.

1 "You do not have to spend a lot of money to look great."

2 "If you think you look good in something, you almost certainly do."

VOCABULARY IN CONTEXT

▶ **2.11** Watch the excerpts from the TED Talk. Choose the correct meaning
of the words.

PRESENTATION SKILLS Using effective body language

> When you give a presentation, your body language is important. Effective body
> language supports your message and shows you are a confident speaker.

A ▶ **2.12** Read the tips about effective body language below. Watch an excerpt from
Arrington's TED Talk. Check [✓] the tips that Arrington follows.

☐ Keep your body open. Try not to cross your arms or legs.

☐ Stand up straight.

☐ Gesture with your hands open.

☐ Make eye contact with the audience.

☐ Smile.

B ▶ **2.12** Watch again. What else does Arrington do (or not do) that shows she's
confident?

C Work in a group. Stand up and tell the group a little about yourself. Try to use effective
body language.

**❝ Confidence is key. If
you think you look good
in something, you almost
certainly do. ❞**

2E Green shopping

COMMUNICATE Are you a green shopper?

A Are you a green shopper? Read the questions below and mark your answers.

How often do you ...	Never	Sometimes	Often
1 buy locally produced products?	☐	☑	☐
2 bring a reusable cloth bag to a store?	☐	☑	☐
3 buy products made from recycled materials?	☑	☐	☐
4 buy secondhand items?	☑	☑	☐
5 donate to charity stores?	☐	☑	☐
6 recycle the packaging that comes with your products?	☐	☑	☐
7 travel to the shops by car?	☐	☐	☑

B Work with a partner. Take turns asking and answering the questions. Circle your partner's answers.

C Look back at the answers. Circle how green you think your partner is.

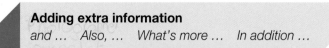

| very green | pretty green | somewhat green | not very green |

D Work in a group. Tell your group how green you think your partner is. Give reasons.

> **Adding extra information**
> *and ... Also, ... What's more ... In addition ...*

WRITING Social media post

A Read the post.

> Help! I want to buy some secondhand items, such as clothes, music, comic books, and furniture. Where's a good place to shop? All ideas welcome. Thanks!

B Write a response to the post. Answer these questions.

What is the name of the store?   How often do you go there?

What do they sell?   What do you like about it?

> For furniture, there's a great store in Plaza Mall. It's called Couch Potato. They sell cheap secondhand furniture. I usually go there during the week when it's not so busy.

3 Career Paths

" So, surf photographer, right? I don't even know if it's a real job title, to be honest. **"**

Chris Burkard
Surf photographer, TED speaker

UNIT GOALS

In this unit, you will …

- talk about types of jobs.
- read about people who changed their job.
- watch a TED Talk about an unusual job.

WARM UP

▶ **3.1** Watch part of Chris Burkard's TED Talk. Answer the questions with a partner.

1 What do you think Burkard's job is like? *Photographer*

2 Look through the unit. What other jobs do you see? Which are the most interesting to you?

French chef Eric Cros shows students how to prepare lamb and vegetables.

3A What do you do?

VOCABULARY Jobs

A ▶ **3.2** Complete the sentences using the words in the box. Watch and check your answers.

chef ✓	dancer	journalist ✓	photographer ✓
pilot ✓	professor ✓	scientist ✓	waiter

1 A _Photographer_ takes pictures with a camera.
2 A _journalist_ writes for a newspaper.
3 A _professor_ gives lectures at a university.
4 A _Pilot_ flies airplanes.

5 A _chef_ creates meals for a restaurant.
6 A _waiter_ performs on a stage. _dancer_
7 A _scientist_ does experiments.
8 A _chef_ serves food and drinks.

B Write each job from **A** under one of the headings below.

Education and Research	News and Media	Entertainment	Travel	Stores and Restaurants
Professor scientist coach. instructor	Photographer Journalist.	dancer Artis actor Singer model. influencer	Pilot. Model	chef waiter recepcion.

C Work with a partner. Think of and add one more job for each heading.

Another job in Education and Research is teacher.

Good one. How about News and Media?

LISTENING Interview with a TV presenter

> **Listening selectively**
> You may not understand every word when people speak. Listen selectively and focus on the key information you need.

A ▶ **3.3** Richard Lenton is a journalist and TV presenter. Watch and check [✓] the topics he talks about.

- ☐ the best things about his job
- ☐ his future hopes
- ☐ the challenges in his job
- ☐ his free time

B ▶ **3.3** Watch again. Circle the correct words.

1 Lenton usually presents (**soccer** / **tennis**) shows.

2 Lenton (**likes** / **doesn't like**) presenting live TV shows.

3 Presenting on the World Cup was challenging because of (**his studio guests** / **the hours**).

4 Lenton usually plays soccer (**once** / **twice**) a week.

Richard Lenton (right) interviews David Beckham.

C CRITICAL THINKING

Personalizing Discuss with a partner. Do you think you would be a good TV presenter? Why or why not?

SPEAKING Talking about jobs

A ▶ **3.4** Does speaker B like his new job?

A: So, how do you like being a barista?

B: Oh, it's great! ⸺⸺⸺⸺ fantastic / excellent

A: Yeah? What do you do every day?

B: Well, you know, I make coffee and serve it to customers.

A: Is it hard work? ⸺⸺⸺⸺ difficult / tough

B: Sometimes. The hours aren't great, but I don't mind. The pay isn't / The boss isn't

A: Isn't it boring?

B: No, it's really fun. I meet a lot of cool people. ⸺⸺⸺ interesting / enjoyable

B Practice the conversation with a partner. Practice again using the words on the right.

C Imagine you have a new job. Choose one from this lesson or think of your own.

Work with a partner. Ask each other about your jobs.

> I'm a chef at China Bistro.

> Great! How do you like it?

3B What job would you like?

LANGUAGE FOCUS Discussing job preferences

A ▶ 3.5 Read the information. Is the information surprising?

1 Pilot

TOP 10
DREAM JOBS

A recent survey asked 3,000 workers in the U.K. to name their dream job. For most people, the perfect job is a pilot. Others prefer jobs in the arts—such as a writer or an actor—or as a sportsperson.

2 Charity worker

3 Writer

4 Photographer

5 Musician

6 Sports trainer

7 Race car driver

8 Actor

9 Journalist

10 Artist

B ▶ 3.6 Two people are talking about their jobs. Watch and complete the sentences.

The woman works as a(n) _Jornalist_. She doesn't like the _hoor 7pm_. 8pm
She'd like to be a(n) _charity worker_.

C ▶ 3.7 Watch and study the language in the chart.

Asking about and describing jobs	
Do you have a job?	Yes, I do. No, I don't. I'm a student.
What do you do?	I'm a manager. I work in marketing.
What's your job like?	It's (really) fun. It's (pretty) easy.
What do you like about your job? What don't you like about your job?	The pay is great. I don't like the hours. They're terrible.
What (kind of) job would you like to have (someday)?	I'd like to be a charity worker.

For more information on **like vs. would like**, see Grammar Summary 3 on page 155.

D Match each question to the best response.

1 Do you have a job? — Yes, I do.

2 What do you do? — I'm a fashion designer.

3 What's your job like? — It's pretty easy.

4 What don't you like about your job? — My boss isn't great.

5 What job would you like to have someday? — I'd love to write for a magazine.

E ▶ **3.8** Complete the information. Circle the correct words. Listen and check your answers.

Many people ¹(**do** /**would**) like to work as a pilot one day. According to one survey, in the U.K., it's the number one dream job. But what's the job really ²(**like** /**love**)? A good point is you can travel to a lot of interesting places — for free. The pay is ³(**like** /**pretty**) good, too. So what don't pilots like ⁴(**for** /**about**) their job? The hours ⁵(**are** /**is**) not great — they're often away from home and spend a lot of time in hotels. Pilots often ⁶(**work** /**works**) on holidays, too, as those are the busiest days for flying.

Ethiopian Airlines' first female captain Amsale Gualu prepares for takeoff

SPEAKING A future job

A Think of two possible jobs you'd like to have someday. Use jobs from the chart on page 36 or your own ideas. Write your ideas below.

	Job 1	Job 2
A job I'd like to have	travels fles Ahigh addenti	good programs in the compute marhentlg
Why I want it		desiner a good marheting for thes company

B Work in a group. Share your ideas.

I'd love to be a chef.

Why is that?

Because I love to cook and I like working in a team.

Misty Copeland performing for the American Ballet Theater

3C A dancer's dream

PRE-READING Predicting

A Look at the lesson title, photo, and caption. What do you think the passage is mainly about?

    a why it is important to start ballet training early

    b the challenges someone had before she became a dancer

    c the reason more boys are becoming interested in ballet

B Read the passage. Check your prediction.

▶ 3.9

An athletic young woman turns, and spins, and leaps. In the background, a young girl reads a rejection[1] letter from a ballet school. "You have the wrong body for ballet," it says, "and
5 at thirteen, you are too old." This was one of the most popular advertisements of 2014, and features American Ballet Theater principal[2] dancer Misty Copeland.

This was not a real letter. But Copeland says it
10 is very similar to letters from her childhood. While many dancers start at the age of 3, Copeland only began to study ballet as a 13-year-old. People often told her that she was too old, or that she didn't have the **perfect** body type (she is only 157 cm
15 tall). Her family moved a lot, and it was sometimes a **struggle** to attend ballet classes.

But Copeland loved dancing and did not want to **quit**. She stayed with her ballet teacher on weekdays and **spent time** with her family only on
20 weekends. This was a difficult **routine**, but she worked hard and at age 14 won her first national competition.[3] Copeland joined the American Ballet Theater in 2000 and performed in many ballets over the next few years. In 2007, she became
25 a solo[4] performer, and in 2015, she became its principal dancer.

Copeland is now a dancer, author, and Broadway performer. She also stars in the 2015 movie *A Ballerina's Tale*. So what's next? According
30 to Copeland, anything is possible. "My **career** really is just now beginning."

---

[1] **rejection:** *n.* not accepting
[2] **principal:** *adj.* first in order of importance

[3] **competition:** *n.* an event to find out who is the best at something
[4] **solo:** *adj.* done alone, not with other people

UNDERSTANDING SEQUENCE

Complete the timeline with information about Misty Copeland.

	wins a national 2 _____ for the first time			becomes a 4 _____ performer	

1982	**1995**	**1996**	3 _____	**2007**	**2015**

is born

starts to learn ballet as a 1 _____ -year-old

becomes a member of the American Ballet Theater

becomes the principal dancer and stars in a 5 _____

UNDERSTANDING DETAILS

Check [✓] the challenges below that are mentioned in the reading.

- ☐ Many people told Copeland she was too old to start ballet.
- ☐ Copeland's family did not have enough money to pay for ballet classes.
- ☐ Many people said Copeland had the wrong body type to be a ballerina.
- ☐ Copeland's family moved often, so it was difficult to go to ballet classes.
- ☐ Copeland did not have enough time to do her schoolwork.
- ☐ Copeland had to spend a lot of time away from her family.

BUILDING VOCABULARY

A Match the words in **blue** from the passage to their definitions.

1 **perfect** ○	○ good in every way
2 **struggle** ○	○ the things you usually do
3 **routine** ○	○ something that is very difficult to do

B Choose the correct option to complete the sentences.

1 If you **quit** something, you _____ doing it.
   a start
   b stop

2 An example of a **career** is working _____.
   a in a part-time summer job
   b as a full-time business manager

3 If you **spend time** with your friends, you _____.
   a do things together
   b buy things for them

C **CRITICAL THINKING**

Evaluating Which of Misty Copeland's **struggles** do you think was the biggest challenge? Discuss with a partner.

3D The joy of surfing in ice-cold water

TEDTALKS

CHRIS BURKARD is a surf photographer, but you won't find him working on a warm **exotic** island. Instead, he prefers the Arctic, with its **rough** seas and **freezing** temperatures. His idea worth spreading is that anything worth pursuing is likely to involve a struggle, but the joy that results far outweighs the **suffering**.

PREVIEWING

Read the paragraph above. Match each **bold** word to its meaning. You will hear these words in the TED Talk.

1 very cold: _____

2 not calm: _____

3 unusual or different: _____

4 feeling of pain: _____

VIEWING

A ▶ **3.10** Watch Part 1 of the TED Talk and answer the questions.

1 Where is Burkard in the photo?

   a Canada   **b** Iceland   **c** Norway

2 How does he describe the water?

   a beautiful   **b** freezing   **c** rough

B ▶ **3.11** Watch Part 2 of the TED Talk. Order the events in Burkard's life from 1 to 4.

_____ He begins to work in cold places.

_____ He begins to work in warm places.

_____ He becomes bored with his job.

_____ He learns that sometimes achieving our dreams involves a struggle.

C CRITICAL THINKING

Personalizing **Work with a partner. Discuss answers to these questions.**

1 Why does Burkard like his job?

2 Would you like to be a surf photographer? Why or why not?

VOCABULARY IN CONTEXT

 3.12 Watch the excerpts from the TED Talk. Choose the correct meaning of the words.

PRESENTATION SKILLS Thanking the audience

> At the end of a presentation, many speakers will thank their audience. It's polite, and it also lets the audience know that you've finished.

A ▶ **3.13** Watch the excerpt. Write the phrase Burkard uses to thank the audience.

_____

B ▶ **3.14** Watch two excerpts from the TED Talks from Units 1 and 2. Check [✓] how the speakers thank their audience.

	"Thank you."	"Thank you so much."	"Thank you very much."
Sleepy Man Banjo Boys			
Jessi Arrington			

C Work in a group. Think of other ways to thank the audience.

“ Why would anyone ever want to surf in freezing cold water? **”**

3E Job descriptions

COMMUNICATE What's my job?

A Look at the jobs in the box. Check any you don't know in your dictionary.

airplane pilot	café barista	dog trainer	graphic artist
movie actor	photojournalist	professional athlete	songwriter
surfing instructor	TV chef	university professor	video game designer

B ▶ **3.15** Listen to five sentences describing one of the jobs above. After each sentence, try to guess which job it is.

C **Student A**: turn to page 141. **Student B**: turn to page 144. Read the sentences and guess your partner's job.

> OK, number one: I usually work inside ...

> Are you a barista?

D Now choose another job from this unit. Write five sentences to describe the job.

E Work in groups of 3 or 4. Take turns reading your job descriptions. Your group members must try to guess the job you are describing.

> **Asking for clarification**
>
> *Can you repeat that, please?*   *Sorry, what did you say?*   *Can you say that again?*

WRITING Describing a dream job

Imagine you have your dream job. Write about what you do, and why you like it.

> I work as a dog trainer. I teach dogs to behave well and follow instructions. It's fun but challenging. I enjoy it because I love animals and I enjoy meeting new people, too.

Presentation 1

MODEL PRESENTATION

A Complete the transcript of the presentation using the words in the box.

tell	work	favorite	much
people	goes	works	name

"Hi. My ¹_____'s Paula. I'd like to ²_____
you a bit about my brother, Zak. He's 21 and he's a university
student. He also ³_____ part-time as a barista. The
pay isn't great and he says it's hard ⁴_____ but he
really enjoys it. He also really loves fashion and shopping for clothes.
He ⁵_____ shopping every weekend and his
⁶_____ shop is Uniqlo. He has an interesting hobby, too.
He's an actor for a local theater group. He really loves acting—he says
it's fun and he meets a lot of ⁷_____. One day, he'd like
to write his own plays. OK, so that's my brother Zak!
Thank you so ⁸_____ for listening."

B ▶ **P.1** Watch the presentation and check your answers.

C ▶ **P.1** Review the list of presentation skills from Units 1–3 below. Which does the speaker use? Check [✓] each skill used as you watch again.

The speaker …
- introduces herself ☐
- smiles ☐
- stands up straight ☐
- makes eye contact ☐
- thanks the audience ☐

D Look at the notes Paula made before her presentation. Did she forget to say anything?

- Introduction: my name / topic
- Zak: 21 / student / studies Art
- His job: barista / pay / hard work / enjoy
- Likes: fashion / shopping every weekend / Uniqlo
- Hobby: actor / theater group / fun / meets people
- Dreams: write own play / star in a movie
- End: thank audience

YOUR TURN

A You are going to plan and give a short presentation to a partner introducing someone you know. Use Paula's notes above for ideas and include any other information. Make notes on a card or a small piece of paper.

B Look at the useful phrases in the box below. Think about which ones you will need in your presentation.

Useful phrases	
Introducing yourself:	(Informally) *I'm/My name's …*
	(Formally) *I want/I'd like to introduce myself. I'm / My name's …*
Introducing your topic:	*I'd like to (tell you/talk to you) about …*
Describing likes/favorites:	*He/She really likes/loves / enjoys …*
	His/her favorite _____ is …
Describing routines:	*He/She _____ every week / twice a month*
Describing hopes:	*One day, (he'd/she'd) like to _____*
Ending:	*Thank you so much (for listening).*
	Thanks for listening.

C Work with a partner. Take turns giving your presentation using your notes. Use some of the presentation skills from units 1–3. As you listen, check [✓] each skill your partner uses.

The speaker …
- introduces himself/herself ☐
- smiles ☐
- stands up straight ☐
- makes eye contact ☐
- thanks the audience ☐

D Give your partner some feedback on their talk. Include two things you liked, and one thing he or she can improve.

> Well done! You introduced yourself, and you smiled a lot. But you didn't make eye contact enough.

4 Talents

" I'd like to give you guys a bit of a demonstration about what I do. "

Tom Thum
Beatboxer, TED speaker

UNIT GOALS

In this unit, you will …

- talk about abilities and talents.
- read about an unusual career.
- watch a TED Talk about turning an unusual talent into a career.

WARM UP

▶ **4.1** Watch part of Tom Thum's TED Talk. Answer the questions with a partner.

1 How would you describe Thum's performance?

2 Look through this unit. What other talents do you see?

A contestant finishes his sand sculpture during a competition at Revere Beach in the United States.

4A What are you good at?

VOCABULARY Abilities

A Look at the abilities. ~~Cross out~~ the option that doesn't belong.

1 playing	friends	soccer	video games
2 taking	photos	tests	presentations
3 making	decisions	photos	friends
4 giving	advice	decisions	presentations

B Choose six abilities from **A**. How good are you at each of them? Add them to the scale below. Then add two more abilities.

← Really bad   Not very good   Good   Pretty good   Very good →

C Work with a partner. Share your information.

> I'm pretty good at playing soccer. How about you?

> I'm not very good at playing soccer.

46

LISTENING A unique ability

> **Recognizing unstressed words**
> Native speakers do not stress every word they say. It's important to be able to recognize the sounds of unstressed words. For example, the word "can" is usually not stressed.

A ▶ **4.2** Okotanpe is a contact juggler. Watch and circle the correct option.

Contact jugglers can …

   a play the piano and juggle.   **b** roll balls on their bodies.   **c** juggle with bubbles.

B ▶ **4.2** Watch again. Circle **T** for true or **F** for false.

   1 Many people watched Okotanpe on YouTube.   **T**   **F**

   2 The balls are very soft.   **T**   **F**

   3 Okotanpe practices every day.   **T**   **F**

   4 Okotanpe can also do magic tricks.   **T**   **F**

C **CRITICAL THINKING**

   Reflecting Do you think contact juggling is more difficult than regular juggling? Why or why not? Discuss with a partner.

Okotanpe is a contact juggler from Japan.

SPEAKING Talking about abilities

A ▶ **4.3** What is speaker B good at?

   A: Wow! You're pretty good.   really good / not bad

   B: Thanks. I practice a lot.

   A: Can you play any other instruments?

   B: Well, I can play the guitar—but I'm not very good at it.   so good / that good

   A: Do you know how to read music?

   B: Actually, no. I'm really bad at it.   hopeless / terrible

   A: Really? So how do you learn the songs?

   B: I usually just listen and then try to play what I hear.

   A: Wow! That's amazing.   great / fantastic

B Practice the conversation with a partner. Practice again using the words on the right.

C Write two true and two false statements about things you are good at. Work in a group. Share your information. Can others guess which statements are false?

   OK, I'll go first. I'm really good at singing.

   Hmm. I think that's true.

   Sorry, you're wrong. I'm really bad at it.

4B What talents do you have?

LANGUAGE FOCUS Describing talents and abilities

A ▶ **4.4** Read the information. Which of these jobs do you think you can do?

TURNING TALENT INTO CASH
Do you have a unique talent? There's a job out there waiting for you!

Pearl diver
Are you good at swimming underwater? Can you hold your breath for a long time? Pearl divers earn their money by collecting pearls from the bottom of the sea.

Human statue
Perhaps your only ability is that you can stand perfectly still. Well, there's still a job for you! You can get paid for dressing up as a statue in public as part of promotional events.

Odor tester
Some people even make a career out of a good sense of smell. Odor testers make a living by testing the smell of things like perfumes and deodorants.

Voice artist
If you can speak in different, funny voices, how about becoming a voice artist? Providing voices for characters in animations can get you a pretty good salary.

B ▶ **4.5** Two people are talking about the jobs above. Watch and complete the sentences.

1 The woman can't ___swiming   underwater___ very well.

2 The man thinks he could become a(n) _____.

C ▶ **4.6** Watch and study the language in the chart.

Describing abilities and talents		
Are you good at	languages? writing essays?	Yes, I am. No, I'm not.
Do you know how to	read Japanese? speak Spanish?	Yes, I do. No, I don't.
Can you	play a musical instrument? ride a bike?	Yes, I can. No, I can't.
What abilities or talents do you have?	I can	run quickly. speak Spanish fluently. solve word problems easily. read Korean well.

For more information on **can** and **can't**, see Grammar Summary 4 on page 156.

D Complete each question with one word.

1 Do you _know_ how to say hello in Chinese?

2 Are you _good_ at writing essays?

3 _do_ _Can_ you hold your breath for one minute?

4 Are you good _at_ swimming underwater?

5 _do_ you play a musical instrument?

6 Do you know _how_ to count to ten in Spanish?

E Work with a partner. Take turns asking the questions in **D**. Answer with your own information.

F ▶ **4.7** Complete the information using the words in the box. One word is extra. Listen and check your answers.

can	easily	do	good	doing	well

Arthur Benjamin is a math professor. But he also has a second job—as a "mathemagician."

As you can guess, Benjamin is very ¹ _good_ at math. But he also knows how to ² _do_ magic, and he combines his two passions into amazing performances.

Benjamin is really good at ³ _doing_ difficult math quickly. During his performances, Benjamin invites audience members with calculators on stage. He races them to see who ⁴ _can_ solve a difficult math problem first. Benjamin wins ⁵ _easily_ almost every time.

Arthur Benjamin performs "mathemagic."

SPEAKING A talented class

A Complete the list of questions below with two more unusual abilities or talents.

Can you say the alphabet backward?		No
Can you stand on one foot for 20 seconds?		Yes
Do you know how to say hello in French?		NO
Can you touch your toes without bending your knees?		N O
Do you know how to sing "Happy Birthday" in English?		N O
Do you know how to _ride in a bike without your hands_?		Yes
Can you _dance the macarena_?		Yes

B Walk around the class and ask the questions. Make the person *show* you the ability. Write the names of people who have the abilities. Get a different name for each talent.

> OK, can you say the alphabet backward?

> Yeah, I think so. Watch me. I'll show you.

Fans watch a StarCraft II tournament in Seoul, South Korea.

4C Pro gaming: a dream career?

PRE-READING Predicting

A Look at the title and subheadings. What do you think the text is mainly about?

    a the life and career of a famous pro gamer

    b how pro gaming is the dream job for many teenagers

    c what it's really like to be a pro gamer

B Skim the reading. Check your prediction.

▶ 4.8

1 Getting paid for playing video games seems like a dream career for many of today's teenagers. But is it all fun and games?

2 **Big business**
Pro gaming is certainly big business. In 2015, there were more than 3,000 gaming **tournaments** and over 10,000 professional players worldwide. Many tournaments attract huge online audiences, and successful gamers can earn millions of dollars from prize money and **advertisements**. The industry is clearly thriving.[1]

3 **What it takes**
Becoming a professional is not just about being good at playing games—it also takes a lot of hard work. Some pro gamers practice for 14 hours a day. "You need to dedicate pretty much your whole life to it," says ex-gamer George "HotshotGG" Georgallidis.

4 **Not all fun and games**
It can be a difficult job as well. **Stress** is a big issue for gamers. Fatigue[2] is another, and **injuries** are common. Top player Hai Lam suffered wrist[3] problems after years of pro gaming. Careers are short, and many gamers **retire** before they are 30 and struggle to find another job.

5 The downsides, however, are unlikely to change the dreams of many teenage gamers. And angry parents are still likely to hear the excuse:[4] "But I'm just practicing for my future job!"

---

[1] **thrive:** *v.* to do well
[2] **fatigue:** *n.* being extremely tired
[3] **wrist:** *n.* the joint between your hand and your arm
[4] **excuse:** *n.* a reason to explain why you did something wrong

UNDERSTANDING PURPOSE

Choose the option that describes the main purpose of each paragraph.

Paragraph 2

a to describe how pro gaming tournaments work

b to show how big the pro gaming industry is these days

Paragraph 3

a to explain how pro gamers practice for major tournaments

b to describe the hard work needed to be a pro gamer

Paragraph 4

a to describe the difficult parts of being a pro gamer

b to explain the career of a retired pro gamer

UNDERSTANDING SUPPORTING DETAILS

Find and underline the following supporting details in the reading.

1 three examples of how pro gaming is now "big business"

2 the amount of practice some pro gamers do

3 three examples of the difficult parts of being a pro gamer

BUILDING VOCABULARY

A Complete the summary using the words in the box below.

advertisements	injuries	retire	stress	tournaments

lessones

A career as a pro gamer

Advantages	Disadvantages
• You can earn a lot of money by winning ¹ tournaments and through ² advertisements. • You can have a career doing something you love.	• You need to practice a lot. • Some gamers get ³ injuries that stop them from playing. • Many pro gamers have to ⁴ retire early and find another job. • ⁵ stress is also a problem for many pro gamers.

B CRITICAL THINKING

Evaluating Do you think professional gaming is a good career choice? Why or why not? Discuss with a partner.

> I think it's a good career choice because …

4D The orchestra in my mouth

TEDTALKS

TOM THUM has an interesting talent. He is a beatboxer. This means he can make unusual **sounds** with his **voice**. His idea worth spreading is that our talents can **allow** us to **pursue** amazing and sometimes surprising careers.

PREVIEWING

Read the paragraph above. Match each **bold** word to its meaning. You will hear these words in the TED Talk.

1 follow: _____

2 the sound when you speak: _____

3 what we hear: _____

4 let: _____

VIEWING

A ▶ **4.9** Watch Part 1 of the TED Talk. Circle the correct words to complete the sentences.

1 Tom Thum makes sounds using (**his voice alone** / **his voice and microphone effects**).

2 Tom Thum comes from (**Brisbane** / **Sydney**), Australia.

B ▶ **4.10** Watch Part 2 of the TED Talk. Check [✓] the things that Thum says the technology allows him to do.

☐ sound like a musical instrument

☐ mix sounds together

☐ play his voice backward

☐ play his voice over and over again

C ▶ **4.11** Watch Part 3 of the TED Talk. What kind of music does Thum perform?

D **CRITICAL THINKING**

Synthesis Who do you think is more talented—Tom Thum or Sleepy Man Banjo Boys? Discuss with a partner.

VOCABULARY IN CONTEXT

▶ **4.12** Watch the excerpts from the TED Talk. Choose the correct meaning of the words.

PRESENTATION SKILLS Introducing a topic

> Introducing your topic helps the audience know what to expect and helps the speaker structure the talk. Here are some useful phrases.
>
> I'm going to discuss …   I'd like to share with you …
> I want to show you …   I'd love to give you some perspective on …
> I want to tell you about …   I'd like to give a demonstration of …

A ▶ **4.13** Watch the excerpts from Tom Thum's TED Talk. How does he introduce his topic? Complete the sentences.

1 "I'd _____ to give you guys a bit of a _____ about what I do."

2 "I would _____ to _____ with you some technology that I brought …"

B ▶ **4.14** Complete the sentences from the TED Talks in the previous units. Write **a**, **b**, or **c**. Watch the excerpts to check your answers.

1 **Robbie Mizzone (Sleepy Man Banjo Boys)** "I'm just going to _____."

2 **Jessi Arrington** "I'd really love to _____."

3 **Chris Burkard** "I'd love to _____."

    a give you a little perspective on what a day in my life can look like

    b take a second to introduce the band

    c show you my week's worth of outfits right now

C Choose one of the topics below. Give a one-minute talk on that topic to your partner. Remember to introduce the topic first.

| a talented person you know | a job you'd like | someone who has a job they love |

❝ My name's Tom Thum, and I'm a beatboxer. ❞

4E The right job

COMMUNICATE Recommending a job

A Work with a partner. Read the information below. Then try the roleplay.

Student A: You work for an employment agency. You have jobs to fill. Interview Student B using the questions on page 143. Ask for extra information. Note your partner's answers.

Student B: You need a job. Student A works for an employment agency. Answer his or her questions.

> **Conversation fillers**
>
> *Well ...*   *Um ...*   *Let's see ...*   *Hmm ...*

B Now switch roles.

C Turn to page 143 and look at the list of job vacancies. Think about your partner's abilities and preferences. Find two or more jobs that are suitable for your partner.

D Recommend the jobs to your partner. Say why you think each job is good for him or her. Does your partner agree?

> Underwater photographer is a good job for you. You said you're good with animals, and you can swim well.

> OK, yes, that sounds interesting. Anything else?

WRITING Describing an unusual ability

A Think about the people you know. Who has an unusual ability or talent?

Person: _____   Ability/Talent: _____

B Write a paragraph about the person.

> My uncle is very talented. He can play the bagpipes. They are a traditional musical instrument from Scotland. He sometimes plays them at birthday parties or other events, but he usually just plays them for fun.

5 Technology

> **"** I don't have feathers. But I feel like a bird sometimes. **"**

Yves Rossy
Jetman, TED speaker

UNIT GOALS

In this unit, you will ...

- talk about how technology affects our lives.
- read about how a new technology allows a person to fly.
- watch a TED Talk about the excitement and challenges of flying.

WARM UP

▶ **5.1** Watch part of Yves Rossy's TED Talk. Answer the questions with a partner.

1 Would you like to fly like Rossy? Why or why not?

2 How is this different from other types of flying?

More and more people now own a personal drone.

5A It's the latest thing.

VOCABULARY Gadgets

A Read the paragraphs below. Then write each **bold** word next to its opposite.

Most smartwatches have a very cool, **modern** design. They're **easy to use** and link with your smartphone so you get all your messages as **fast** as possible.	While many people still buy books, others prefer e-readers. Recent models are extremely **light** and **thin**, but they're also very **strong**. You can download books directly to your device.	Personal drones are becoming more and more popular. They're great **fun** and easy to fly. But they can be **expensive**—from $500 on up.

1 boring ≠ _fun_
2 cheap ≠ _expensive_
3 difficult to use ≠ _easy to use_
4 heavy ≠ _light_

5 old-fashioned ≠ _modern_
6 slow ≠ _fast_
7 thick ≠ _thin_
8 weak ≠ _strong_

B How important are these gadgets to you? Mark your opinion about each one.

> 1 = I can't live without mine.   3 = I'd like to get one.
> 2 = I like having one.   4 = I don't need one.

_1_ a smartphone 1
_4_ a game console 3
_3_ a tablet   4
_3_ an e-reader   2.

_1_ a smart TV   4
_4_ a smartwatch
_4_ a personal drone
_3_ a universal remote

C Work with a partner. Share your ideas.

I can't live without my game console.

Really? I don't need one. I play games on my tablet.

LISTENING How I used drones to make an amazing video

> **Listening for attitude**
> In order to understand a speaker's attitude or opinion about something, listen for positive or negative words or phrases. Sometimes a speaker's tone can also give you a clue.

A ▶ **5.2** Sam Cossman is an explorer and filmmaker. What did he study in Vanuatu? Watch and circle the correct answer.

  a a giant cave   **b** a volcano   **c** a temple

B Watch again. Circle the correct options.

  1 Cossman used drones to (**take images** / **measure the temperature**).

  2 Some drones were destroyed because of the (**strong winds** / **heat**).

  3 Cossman also used a special (**suit** / **car**) to get close.

  4 Cossman said he (**was** / **wasn't**) afraid during his experience.

C **CRITICAL THINKING**

  Applying What else could drones help to study? Discuss with a partner.

Sam Cossman in Vanuatu

SPEAKING Talking about gadgets

A ▶ **5.3** Why does speaker B like his smartwatch?

  A: Is that a smartwatch?

  B: Yeah.

  A: How do you like it?   How is it? / What do you think of it?

  B: Oh, I love it. It looks cool, and it's really easy to use.   user-friendly / practical

  A: Yeah? What does it do?

  B: Oh, a lot of things. For example, it can connect to   lots of / so many
  my smartphone and send me messages.

  A: Great. How much do they cost?   How much are they? / What do they cost?

  B: This one was $200. But the newer ones cost more.

B Practice the conversation with a partner. Practice again using the words on the right.

C Work with a partner. Choose one gadget that you know about. What do you like or dislike about it? Share your opinions.

  I have a new tablet.

  What do you think of it?

  It's OK. It's really light, but it's not very easy to use.

5B What does it do?

LANGUAGE FOCUS Discussing technology

A ▶ **5.4** Read the information. Which piece of wearable technology would you like to wear?

WEARABLE TECHNOLOGY

Check out the latest wearable gadgets. Some are available now, and others you may use in the future.

Smart glasses
These allow you to record or watch video. They also add useful information to what you see.

Vibrating tattoo
A special substance makes your skin vibrate every time you get a message or call on your cellphone.

GAME VEST

Spray-on clothes
Just spray on your skin and let it dry. You are left with real clothing that you can even wash.

Smart bracelet
The smart bracelet can change color when your friends are nearby. It also lets you know when you get a message on your phone.

Gaming vest
Ouch! Wear it while you play computer games. You feel what it's like when someone hits you.

B ▶ **5.5** Two people are talking about gadgets. Watch and complete the sentences.

1 The woman uses the smart glasses to _____ .

2 The man's fitness band can track his _____ .

C ▶ **5.6** Watch and study the language in the chart.

Describing things and how they work		
What does your smartwatch do?	It can	connect to my smartphone. play music.
What do you use it for?	I use it	to pay for things. to track my heart rate.
How many apps do you have on your smartphone?		Quite a lot. Not many. It's new. Only a few right now.
How much battery life does it have?		Quite a lot. I only charge it at night. Not much. I charge it twice a day. Only a little. I need to recharge it every few hours.

For more information on **quantifiers**, see Grammar Summary 5 on page 156.

D Complete the sentences below. Use your own ideas.

Example: You can use a fitness band _to track your fitness_.

1 You can use a personal drone _to take a beautiful video_.

2 You can use a smartwatch _to texto to offthe pepler or look for cell -phoor_

3 You can use an e-reader _to read the book - differentes_.

4 You can use a universal remote _to change wherever you want_

5 You can use a smart TV _to watching movies, listen to music "entretment"_

E ▶ **5.7** Complete the paragraph. Circle the correct words. Listen and check your answers.

Hoverboards were once seen only in science fiction movies. But now the dream is slowly becoming reality.

[1](**A few**/ Much) companies have now started making them—and they look pretty cool! They use magnets so that the boards can fly just [2](a few /**a little**) centimeters above the ground.

The hoverboards are not perfect, however. They only work on a special surface, so there are not [3](**many**/ much) places you can use them. They're also difficult to use—even pro skaters need [4](many /**a lot of**) practice. And they also cost [5](**a lot of**/ much) money. Still, even at $10,000 each, one company's hoverboards sold out quickly.

The Hendo Hoverboard hovers just above the ground.

SPEAKING Wearable technology

A Work in a group. Look at the items below or think of your own ideas. Discuss how to make them into wearable technology.

| a hat | socks | sneakers | a scarf | a ring | earrings |

B Choose one of your group's ideas. Give the gadget a name and make notes below.

Name:

What does it do?

How does it work?

C Join another group. Share your ideas.

I'd like to tell you about the Smart Ring.

OK. What does it do?

Well, it can connect to my smartphone, and it changes color when I get a text message.

5C Flying like a bird

PRE-READING Predicting

A Work with a partner. Discuss the questions.

1 How do you think Rossy controls his aircraft?

2 How do you think Rossy stays safe when he's flying?

B Read the article. Check your predictions.

" It's really pure flying. "

▶ 5.8

A man stands at the open door of a helicopter, around 2,000 meters above the ground. On his back is a jet-powered "wing." He starts his four **engines** and then jumps from the helicopter, 5 diving toward the ground at great speed. The man arches[1] his back to stop the dive, and now he's flying! This is not a scene from an action movie—it's just another day for the Jetman, Yves Rossy.

"I really have the feeling of being a bird," says 10 Rossy. He has little **equipment** and no controls to help **steer** the wing. He changes his direction simply by moving his body. "It's really pure flying. It's not steering, it's flight." He only has two instruments[2]—one to tell him the current height and 15 another to tell him how much **fuel** he has.

It's a different world from Rossy's previous career as an airline pilot—but safety is still important. If something goes wrong, Rossy has two **parachutes** for himself and another for his wing. If one engine 20 stops, he can continue on three or even two. "So plan B, always a plan B," explains Rossy.

After just less than ten minutes, the fuel is almost empty. Rossy opens his parachute, and he begins to fall gently to the ground. Another successful flight 25 is complete. In the future, Rossy hopes to make this kind of flight safer, and as he says, "I hope it will be for everybody."

[1] **arch:** *v.* to bend into a U-shape
[2] **instrument:** *n.* a type of measuring device

UNDERSTANDING A PROCESS

Look at the diagram. Number the sentences below 1–4.

a _____ He arches his back to stop the dive and starts to fly.

b _____ He stands at the door of a helicopter or an airplane and starts his engines.

c _____ He opens his parachute and lands safely on the ground.

d _____ He jumps and dives toward the ground.

UNDERSTANDING QUOTES

Circle the correct answers.

1 Why does Rossy say, "It's really pure flying"?

  a because he controls his direction using only his body

  b because his wings move up and down like a bird's wings

2 What does Rossy mean when he says, "... plan B, always a plan B"?

  a He became Jetman because he needed another job when his career as a pilot ended.

  b It's important to have another option if something doesn't work.

3 What does Rossy mean when he says, "I hope it will be for everybody"?

  a He hopes everybody enjoys watching him fly.

  b He hopes that everybody will be able to fly like him.

BUILDING VOCABULARY

A Complete the summary using the words in blue from the passage.

> Yves Rossy doesn't need much ¹_____ when he flies. He uses his body to
> ²_____ and uses a ³_____ when he lands. He carries enough
> ⁴_____ to fly for ten minutes. His ⁵_____ give him the speed to
> stay in the air.

B CRITICAL THINKING

Inferring Why do you think Yves Rossy has a parachute for his "wing" as well as for himself?
Discuss with a partner.

5D Fly with the Jetman

TEDTALKS

YVES ROSSY's idea worth spreading is that by integrating our bodies with new technology, we can experience the thrill of "pure" flying. In his unique **aircraft**, he can **climb** to an **altitude** of several thousand meters. He can also go fast—at one-third the **speed** of a passenger plane.

PREVIEWING

A Read the paragraph. Match each **bold** word to its meaning. You will hear these words in the TED.

1 how fast something moves: _speed_

2 planes, helicopters, etc.: _aircraft_

3 height: _altitude_

4 move upward: _climb_

VIEWING

A ▶ **5.9** Watch Part 1 of the TED Talk. What happens when Rossy does these things? Match. There is one extra.

1 He arches his back. ○

2 He pushes his shoulders forward. ○

○ **a** He flies up.

○ **b** He turns.

○ **c** He flies down.

B ▶ **5.10** Watch Part 2 of the Talk. Complete the notes.

1 hundrem milles

What's his top speed?
About ~~55~~ _190_ km/h

What's flying like?
It's fun!
He feels like a _bird_ .

What's the weight of his equipment?
When his equipment is full of fuel, it weighs about _55_ kg.

How did he become Jetman?
Rossy got the idea _20_ years ago when he discovered free falling.

What's next for Jetman?
He wants to teach a _____ guy.
He wants to try taking off from a cliff.

C CRITICAL THINKING

Analyzing Rossy hopes that his kind of flying "will be for everybody" in the future. How does the technology need to improve for this to be possible? Discuss with a partner.

VOCABULARY IN CONTEXT

▶ **5.11** Watch the excerpts from the TED Talk. Choose the correct meaning of the words.

PRESENTATION SKILLS Using gestures effectively

> Gestures can be important when presenting to a group. These tips can help you use gestures effectively.
>
> • Keep your hands relaxed for most of the presentation.
> • Make gestures large enough for your audience to see.
> • Use gestures to make words and ideas easier to understand.

A ▶ **5.12** Watch part of Rossy's talk. Check [✓] the things that he does.

☐ He uses his hands to show how big something is.

☐ He gestures with one hand to the equipment behind him.

☐ He taps his finger against his head to show he is thinking.

☐ He uses his hands to show how the harness goes around him.

B Work with a partner. Read the excerpt below from Chris Burkard's TED Talk. Discuss what kinds of gestures Burkard might make.

"There's only about a third of the Earth's oceans that are warm, and it's really just that thin band around the equator."

C ▶ **5.13** Watch the excerpt. What gestures does Chris Burkard actually make?

❝ It's really an unreal feeling. ❞

5E Great idea!

COMMUNICATE A new app

A Work with a partner. Think of some apps that you use or know about. Discuss what you like about them.

B Think of an idea for a new app. Think about a problem it can solve or how it can make your life easier. Then prepare a short description of the app to try to "sell" the idea to a group of investors.

C Take turns presenting your ideas to the class (the investors). Use gestures to help demonstrate how it works.

> **Responding to ideas**
> *Good idea!*   *That's a great idea!*   *Interesting!*   *Tell me more.*

D Take a class vote. Which app would be the best investment?

WRITING A review

A Think about an item of technology you know, such as an app, a gadget, or video game. List several good points and bad points about it.

Good points	Bad points

B Write a short review of the item to post online.

★ ★ ★ ☆ **Bussapp: Review**

I often use this app for checking buses. It tells me the arrival time of the next bus and how many seats there are. It's very easy to use, but there is one thing I don't like …

---

6 Challenges

> " I do not use my eyes;
> I use my brain. "

Daniel Kish
Perceptual navigation specialist, TED speaker

UNIT GOALS

In this unit, you will …

- talk about challenges you face.
- read about one person's challenges and how he faces them.
- watch a TED Talk about an unusual method of navigating the world.

WARM UP

▶ 6.1 Watch part of Daniel Kish's TED Talk.
Answer the questions with a partner.

1 What challenges do you think Daniel Kish faces?
2 How do you think he deals with those challenges?

A waitress delivers food to customers in a busy restaurant in Memphis, United States.

6A It's a big challenge for me.

VOCABULARY Daily challenges

A ▶ **6.2** Complete the paragraph below using the words in the box. Watch and check your answers.

| friends | health | money | pressure | stress |

It's never been easy growing up, and students today face just as many challenges as previous generations. Many suffer from _____—largely caused by exams and _____ from parents to be successful. Saving _____ is also difficult when you're a full-time student. Some need to take on part-time jobs to pay their tuition fees. And—as it becomes easier for students to study abroad—making _____ in a new country can also be an issue. What's more, all these kinds of worries can sometimes lead to serious _____ problems, such as depression.

B Work with a partner. Write each challenge in **bold** from **A** under one of the headings below. Then add one more challenge for each heading.

It's a big challenge for me.	It's a challenge, but I can deal with it.	It's not a problem for me.

C Work in a group. Share your information.

> Stress from exams is a big challenge for me.

> Me too. But pressure from my parents is not a problem.

LISTENING It's no big deal

A ▶ **6.3** Vasu Sojitra is an adaptive skier. Who taught him to ski? Watch and answer the question.

B ▶ **6.3** Watch again. Circle the correct words.

1 Skiing (**was** / **wasn't**) the first sport Sojitra tried.

2 Skiing in the backcountry is a challenge because (**the snow is thick** / **there are no ski lifts**).

3 Sojitra (**likes** / **doesn't like**) to climb the highest mountains.

4 Sojitra skis (**at the same speed as** / **slower than**) his skiing partners.

C **CRITICAL THINKING**

Personalizing Do you know anyone who faces a similar challenge to Sojitra? Discuss with a partner.

Vasu Sojitra skiing in the United States

SPEAKING Talking about challenges

A ▶ **6.4** What's speaker B's challenge? What does speaker A suggest?

A: So, how do you like your new life here in Spain?

B: Well, it's a great place, but I'm feeling a bit homesick.

A: Oh, I know how you feel. I felt the same when I first moved here.   know what you mean / understand

B: How did you cope?   manage / get through it

A: Well, when you move to a new country, it's really important to try hard to make some new friends. I joined a soccer team.   signed up for / became a member of

B: That's a good idea. I like tennis. Maybe I can find a tennis club.

A: When you join a club, you meet people with similar interests, too.

B: Yeah, I guess you're right. Thanks for the advice.   suggestion / help

B Practice the conversation with a partner. Practice again using the words on the right.

C Think of three challenges you face. Work with a partner. Share your challenges. Say what you do to face them.

I get a lot of pressure from my parents about my grades.

Yeah, that's tough. How do you cope?

6B How do you cope?

LANGUAGE FOCUS Overcoming difficulties

A ▶ **6.5** Look at the ideas for reducing stress. Do you do any of these things? Discuss with a partner.

B ▶ **6.6** Listen to two people talking about the information above. What does the woman do to reduce her stress at exam time? Complete the sentences.

1 Before the exam, she _____ .

2 After the exam, she _____ .

C ▶ **6.7** Listen and study the language in the chart.

Describing sequence	
When I get stressed, I go for a walk. Before the exam starts, I look over my notes one last time. After I finish the exam, I try not to think about it.	
I feel more confident when I'm prepared for an exam. I listen to relaxing music before I take an exam. I always give myself a reward after I take my last exam.	
Before you take an exam, you can do several things.	First, get a good night's sleep. Then, have a light breakfast. Next, try to get to school early. After that, sit alone and relax.

For more information on **time clauses**, see Grammar Summary 6 on page 156.

D Combine the sentences using the words in parentheses.

1 I face any challenge / I try to think of how to solve it (before)

_____

2 I celebrate with my friends / I finish an exam (after)

_____

3 I feel stressed out / my heart starts beating faster (when)

_____

4 I usually ask for help / I don't know how to solve a problem (when)

_____

5 I take three deep breaths / I start any exam (before)

_____

6 I finish a long, stressful day at work / I relax by playing video games (after)

_____

E ▶ **6.8** Complete the information. Circle the correct word in each sentence. Listen and check your answers.

You're sitting in the exam room waiting for your paper. Here are some tips to help you get through the big exam.

1 (**First** / **Before**) you start writing, read all the instructions carefully and slowly. Highlight any important details.

2 (**Then** / **When**), check the back of the paper. Are there any more questions? Many people forget to do this.

3 When you're ready to start, answer the easiest questions (**first** / **next**).

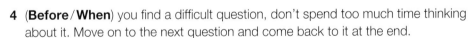

4 (**Before** / **When**) you find a difficult question, don't spend too much time thinking about it. Move on to the next question and come back to it at the end.

5 (**After** / **Before**) you finish, don't leave the room early—check your answers carefully.

F Complete the sentences with your own ideas. Compare with a partner.

1 Before I take a difficult exam, _____ .

2 When I don't know the answer to an exam question, _____ .

3 After I finish an exam, _____ .

4 When I get my exam results, _____ .

SPEAKING Dealing with exam stress

Work in pairs. You are going to teach each other some techniques for dealing with exam stress.
Student A: Turn to page 142. **Student B:** Turn to page 145.

6C Living without fear

PRE-READING Predicting

A Look at the lesson title and photo. What do you think the text is mainly about?

    a how a blind man gets around

    b how new technology is helping blind people see

    c why blind people have good hearing

B Read the passage. Check your prediction.

▶ 6.9

1   Everyone faces challenges in their life, but some are more significant than others. Daniel Kish was born with a type of eye cancer,[1] and doctors **removed** both his eyes before he was 14 months old.

5   Soon after, however, he started to do an amazing thing. He started to make clicking sounds with his tongue to help him move around. Much like a bat,[2] he now moves about using sonar.[3] He is so good at it that he can ride a bicycle by himself on public roads. He and his charity, World Access for the Blind, teach
10 others how to use sonar. In this interview with *National Geographic*, Kish explains how the process works.

1 _____

"When I make a click sound, it makes sound waves.[4] These waves **reflect** off surfaces all around and return to my ears.
15 My **brain** then processes the sound into images. It's like having a conversation with the environment."

2 When you click, what do you see in your mind?
"Each click is like a camera flash. I make a 3-D image of my **surroundings** for hundreds of feet in every direction."

20 **3** _____

"It's thrilling but requires a lot of **focus**. I click up to two times per second, much more than I usually do."

4 Is it dangerous to move around the world in this way?
"Much of the world lives in fear of things that we mostly
25 imagine. I have a habit of climbing anything and everything, but I never broke a bone as a kid."

5 _____

"Many students are surprised how quickly results come. Seeing isn't in the eyes; it's in the mind."

> **❝ Each click is like a camera flash. ❞**

---

[1] **cancer:** *n.* a serious disease where cells that are not normal spread to other parts of the body

[2] **bat:** *n.* a small mammal that flies at night

[3] **sonar:** *n.* a method for locating things (usually underwater) by using sound waves that reflect off objects

[4] **sound waves:** *n.* the form in which sound travels

UNDERSTANDING MAIN IDEAS

Add these questions to the correct blanks in the interview. Write **a**, **b**, or **c**.

   a How challenging is it to teach people to use sonar?

   b What is it like riding a bike using sonar?

   c How does human sonar work?

UNDERSTANDING A PROCESS

How does flash sonar work? Look at the diagram on the right. Number the sentences 1–5.

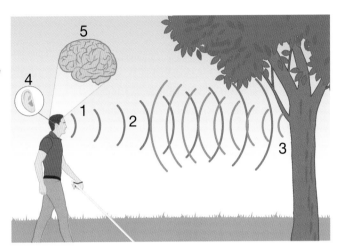

_____ The sound waves reflect off surfaces.

_____ The person makes a clicking sound.

_____ The brain turns the sounds into images.

_____ The sound waves reach the person's ears.

_____ The sound waves travel away from the person.

UNDERSTANDING DETAILS

Circle **T** for true or **F** for false.

1 When Kish clicks, he can "see" for more than a hundred feet. **T**   **F**

2 When Kish rides a bicycle, he clicks less than usual. **T**   **F**

3 As a child, Kish broke his arm when climbing a tree. **T**   **F**

4 Kish's students are usually surprised they can learn so fast. **T**   **F**

BUILDING VOCABULARY

A Match the words in blue from the passage to their definitions.

1 remove ○   ○ the special attention you give to something

2 reflect ○   ○ to take away

3 brain ○   ○ to send back light, sound, etc., from a surface

4 surroundings ○   ○ the part of your body that controls you

5 focus (*n.*) ○   ○ the things around you

B CRITICAL THINKING

Applying How easy do you think the following things are for Daniel Kish to "see" in his surroundings? Discuss with a partner.

a closed door   a road   a moving car   a tree

I think a tree is easy for him to see because the sound waves reflect off it.

Yeah. You're probably right.

6D How I use sonar to navigate the world

TEDTALKS

DANIEL KISH's **remarkable** solution to the challenge of "seeing" while blind has helped many people and **inspired** many others—even those who have not lost their sight. His idea worth spreading is that we all must **face** our challenges, and that we all have the capacity to **navigate** these dark unknowns.

PREVIEWING

A Read the paragraph above. Match each **bold** word to its meaning. You will hear these words in the TED Talk.

1 to find a way: _____

2 amazing: _____

3 try to overcome: _____

4 made to want to do something: _____

B What do you think "these dark unknowns" refers to?

VIEWING

A ▶ 6.10 Work with a partner. Read the excerpt from Daniel Kish's TED Talk and try to guess the missing words. Watch Part 1 of the TED Talk to check your guesses.

"Many of you may have heard me _____ as I came onto the stage … Those are flashes of sound that go out and _____ from surfaces all around me, just like a _____'s sonar, and return to me with patterns, with pieces of information … And my brain, thanks to my parents, has been activated to form images …"

B ▶ 6.11 Watch Part 2 of the TED Talk. Why does Daniel Kish say that he is not "remarkable"?

    a because he has received a lot of help throughout his life

    b because everyone has to overcome challenges using their mind

C ▶ 6.12 Watch Part 3 of the TED Talk. Number the events (1–5) in order to describe the challenge Kish gives to the audience.

    a _____ Kish makes a "shhh" sound and moves the panel to show how the sound changes.

    b _____ Kish holds the panel in front of his face and makes a "shhh" sound.

    c _____ Kish asks the audience to listen again and say "now" when they hear the panel move.

    d _____ Kish asks the audience to close their eyes.

    e _____ The audience hears the panel move and says "now."

D ▶ **6.13** Watch Part 4 of the TED Talk. Circle the correct options to complete the sentences.

1 The video shows people who (**can use flash sonar** / **find it terrifying to be blind**).

2 Kish teaches flash sonar to (**blind** / **blind and sighted**) people from around the world.

E CRITICAL THINKING

Synthesizing What are the similarities between Daniel Kish's ability and Tom Thum's? What are the differences? Discuss with a partner.

VOCABULARY IN CONTEXT

▶ **6.14** Watch the excerpts from the TED Talk. Choose the correct meaning of the words.

PRESENTATION SKILLS Involving your audience

> When giving a presentation, it's important to keep your audience interested. One way of doing this is to involve them in your presentation. For example, you may want to:
>
> Ask the audience to participate in an activity.   Find out about the audience.
> Teach how to do something.   Ask and/or answer questions.

A ▶ **6.15** Watch part of Kish's TED Talk. How does he involve the audience?

a He asks the audience to raise their hands.

b He teaches the audience something.

c He asks the audience to say a word.

B ▶ **6.16** Watch the excerpt of Kish teaching the audience to see with sonar. Then work with a partner and try it. Close your eyes and use your textbook.

❝ I call this process flash sonar. It is how I have learned to see through my blindness. ❞

73

6E Overcoming challenges

COMMUNICATE Dos and don'ts

A Work in a group. Choose one of these everyday challenges, or think of your own. Think about what someone might do to face the challenge.

making friends in a new country	getting good grades
keeping fit	finding a good job
saving money for college	coping with depression

B Create a list of at least 6 tips about how to face the challenge. Write your ideas in the box below.

How to _____

1 _____
2 _____
3 _____
4 _____
5 _____
6 _____

Inviting opinions

What do you think?   *What's your opinion?*   *Do you agree?*

C Now create a poster with your information. Decide what visuals to include. How else can you make your poster interesting? Look back at the infographic on page 68 for ideas.

D Present your poster to the class. Make sure everyone presents part of the poster. Try to involve your audience as much as possible.

WRITING Facing a challenge

Think of someone you know who faced a challenge in their life. Write a paragraph about how they overcame it.

My brother Karl has really bad asthma. When he was younger, it was a real challenge for him. But as he got older, he learned how to deal with it. He plays in a lot of different sports teams at school and he recently won a tennis competition.

Presentation 2

MODEL PRESENTATION

A Complete the transcript of the presentation using the words in the box.

after	watch	quickly	expensive	fun	health
heavy	many	much	play	talk	tell

I'd like to ¹_____ to you about a new piece of technology—a virtual reality headset. How many of you have one? Not so many. Well, I bought mine around a month ago, and I use it quite a lot.

First, I'd like to ²_____ you about the good points. I use it mainly to ³_____ video games. It makes the games much more ⁴_____. It feels very realistic, and it's amazing when you first try it. I also use it to ⁵_____ films, which is really cool.

There are some bad points, though. I'm not sure if it's good for my ⁶_____ or not. Sometimes, ⁷_____ I use it for a long time, I feel a little dizzy for a while. It's also quite ⁸_____, so it's a little uncomfortable to wear for a long time. It was ⁹_____, too—nearly $500—and there aren't ¹⁰_____ games for it right now.

So, would I recommend it? I'd say no, not yet. I think it's best to wait for the price to come down and for the technology to improve. But I think this will happen very ¹¹_____.

Thank you very ¹²_____.

B ▶ **P.2** Watch the presentation and check your answers.

C ▶ **P.2** Review the list of presentation skills from Units 1–6 below. Which does the speaker use? Check [✓] each skill used as you watch again.

The speaker …
- introduces himself ☐
- uses effective body language ☐
- introduces his topic ☐
- uses effective hand gestures ☐
- involves the audience ☐
- thanks the audience ☐

YOUR TURN

A You are going to plan and give a short presentation to a partner introducing a new piece of technology. It could be an app, a gadget, or a video game. Use some or all of the questions below to make some notes.

What is it?

What does it do?

How does it work?

What are the good points about it?

What are the bad points about it?

Would you recommend it to others? Why or why not?

B Look at the useful phrases in the box below. Think about which ones you will need in your presentation.

Useful phrases

Describing how something works:	*It can … / Using it, I can … / I can use it to …*
	It has a lot of … / It doesn't have much/many …
Positive words to describe gadgets:	*modern, easy to use, fast, light, strong, fun, cheap*
Negative words to describe gadgets:	*old-fashioned, difficult to use, slow, heavy, weak, boring, expensive*
Describing sequence:	*When/After I use it, I …*
	To use it, first you need to …
	Then, …

C Work with a partner. Take turns giving your presentation using your notes. Use some of the presentation skills from units 1–6. As you listen, check [✓] each skill your partner uses.

The speaker …
- introduces himself/herself ☐
- uses effective body language ☐
- introduces his topic ☐
- uses effective hand gestures ☐
- involves the audience ☐
- thanks the audience ☐

D Give your partner some feedback on their talk. Include two things you liked, and one thing he or she can improve.

> That was great. Your body language was good, and you involved the audience. But you forgot to thank the audience at the end.

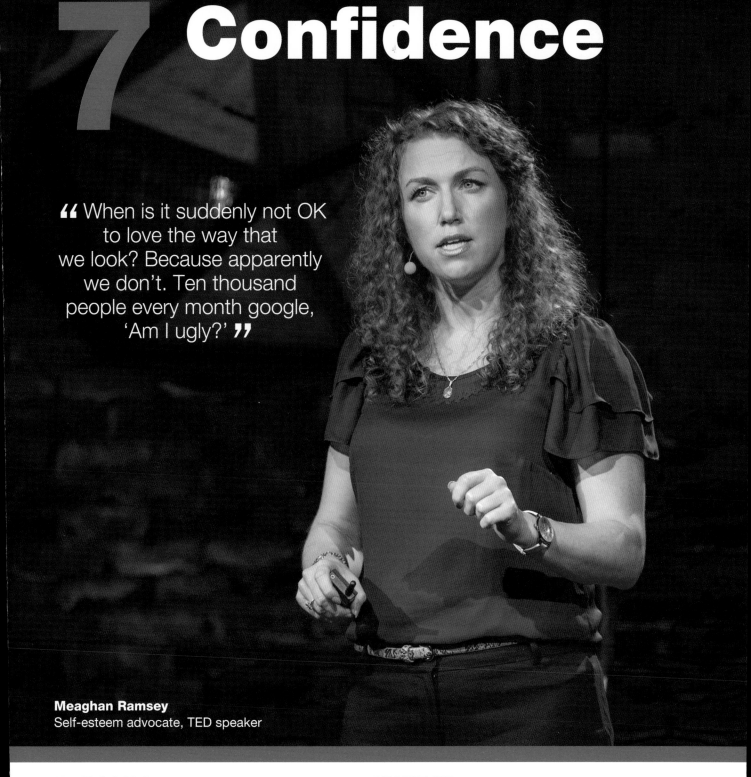

7 Confidence

" When is it suddenly not OK to love the way that we look? Because apparently we don't. Ten thousand people every month google, 'Am I ugly?' **"**

Meaghan Ramsey
Self-esteem advocate, TED speaker

UNIT GOALS

In this unit, you will …

- describe people's appearance and personality.
- read about how the media affects the way we see ourselves.
- watch a TED Talk about the negative effects of low self-esteem.

WARM UP

▶ **7.1** Watch part of Meaghan Ramsey's TED Talk. Answer the questions with a partner.

1 How important do you think appearance is?
2 At what age do you think people start to think about their appearance?

7A He's kind of shy.

VOCABULARY Appearance and personality

A Read the descriptions and add the **bold** words to the correct column.

> " Hi. My name's Kyle. I'm 17 years old and a little **short** for my age. But people say I'm
> **handsome**. I agree! I have two close friends—Nate and Amanda. Nate is kind of **shy**
> and not very **talkative**. But he can be really **funny**. Amanda is **tall** and **thin**. I think she
> looks like a model. Some people say she can be **selfish**, but I don't think so. "

Appearance		Personality	
attractive	heavy	easygoing	smart
beautiful	pretty	honest	unfriendly

B Look at the words in the chart. Which words have a positive meaning? Which have a negative meaning? Discuss with a partner. Are there any words that you don't agree on?

C Look at the image on this page. Work with a partner. Talk about some of the people.

> I think this person is really pretty.

> Yeah. And she looks friendly.

LISTENING Like mother, like daughter

A ▶ **7.2** Bonnie Kim is talking about herself and her mother. Watch and circle the words you hear.

talkative	quiet	shy	funny	easygoing	tall

> **Listening for similarities**
> The following phrases are used to describe similarities.
>
> *We're **both** short.* **Both of us** *like eating out.*
> ***Neither of us** is very tall.* *We look **the same**.*

Bonnie Kim takes a selfie with her mother in Seoul, Korea.

B ▶ **7.2** Watch again. Circle **T** for true or **F** for false.

1 Kim and her mother are both quite tall. **T** **F**

2 Kim is talkative, but her mother is very quiet. **T** **F**

3 Kim and her mother both like sports. **T** **F**

4 Kim and her mother both enjoy cooking. **T** **F**

C CRITICAL THINKING

Personalizing In what ways are you similar to your parents? Discuss with a partner.

SPEAKING Talking about family

A ▶ **7.3** How are speaker B and his father similar?

A: Wow, that's a great photo! Is that your dad?

B: Yeah.

A: You look just like him. exactly / a lot

B: Do you think so?

A: Yeah, you have the same nose. eyes / mouth

B: I guess so. But we have really different personalities.

A: Really? What's he like?

B: Well, he's really talkative, but I'm a little quiet. a bit / fairly

A: And I guess that's your mom. She looks really nice. happy / friendly

B: Yeah, she is. Everyone loves my mom.

B Practice the conversation with a partner. Practice again using the words on the right.

C Write below the names of four members of your family. Work with a partner.
Ask each other about the people on your lists.

_____ _____ _____ _____

What's your sister like?

She's really easygoing and fun.

7B He thinks he's too tall.

LANGUAGE FOCUS Describing appearance and personality

A ▶ 7.4 Read the information. Is your country mentioned? If not, how do you think it compares?

HOW **HAPPY** ARE YOU WITH THE WAY YOU **LOOK**?

Tens of thousands of people from around the world recently answered this question.
According to the results, Mexicans are the happiest with the way they look.

The **5** HAPPIEST countries

% of people who are happy with how they look

1. Mexico **74%**
2. Turkey **71%**
3. Ukraine **65%**
4. Brazil **65%**
5. Argentina **62%**

The **5** UNHAPPIEST countries

% of people who are unhappy with the way they look

1. Japan **38%**
2. United Kingdom **20%**
3. South Korea **19%**
4. Australia **19%**
5. Poland **17%**

B ▶ 7.5 An expert is talking about the survey. Watch and circle the correct option.

1 In the survey, responses from men and women were very (**similar** / **different**).

2 12% of both men and women said they were (**extremely** / **fairly**) happy with the way they look.

3 14% of women said they were (**not very happy** / **not happy at all**) with the way they look.

C ▶ 7.6 Watch and study the language in the chart.

Describing people			
What's she like?	She's	extremely very / really pretty quite	talkative. friendly. easygoing. shy.
What does he look like?	He's	kind of / sort of a bit / a little not very	short. heavy. tall.
	He	doesn't look old	at all.
He thinks he's too short.	He thinks he's not tall enough.		

For more information on **modifying adverbs**, see Grammar Summary 7 on page 157.

D Unscramble the words to make sentences.

1 honest / not / is / Lucia / very _____

2 smart / pretty / Paul / is _____

3 is / of / short / Chris / kind _____

4 all / isn't / Richard / friendly / at _____

5 I / short / is / hair / my / too / think _____

6 thinks / enough / not / thin / Jack / he's _____

E Match the sentences that have a similar meaning.

1 He's too young. ○   ○ He's not very old.

He's pretty young. ○   ○ He's not old enough.

2 He's really unfriendly. ○   ○ He's not friendly at all.

He's a bit unfriendly. ○   ○ He's a little unfriendly.

3 He's kind of talkative. ○   ○ He's really talkative.

He's extremely talkative. ○   ○ He's fairly talkative.

F ▶ **7.7** Complete the information. Circle the correct words. Listen and check your answers.

Poor body image is not just a problem for women. Many men are also ¹(**fairly** / **enough**) unhappy with the way they look—and experts believe the problem is getting worse. Like many women, some men believe that they are ²(**too** / **at all**) heavy. But many others believe that they are ³(**enough** / **too**) thin and not muscular ⁴(**enough** / **too**). As a result, there are more men these days who develop serious health problems because of their body image issues. What's also ⁵(**very** / **too**) worrying is that men who suffer with these problems are less likely than women to talk to somebody about it.

SPEAKING A movie of your life

A Imagine you are making a movie about your life so far. Write the names of four important people from your life. These people will be the main characters in your movie.

_____   _____   _____   _____

B Now think about which actors or actresses you'd like to play the different characters. Think about their appearance, age, and personality. Explain your choices to a partner.

> I'd like Tom Cruise to play me. He's quite short, and he's extremely handsome.

> OK. But he's too old now. You're only 22!

7C Pressure to be "perfect"

PRE-READING Previewing

A Read the first paragraph of the article. What problem is mentioned? What do you think causes this problem? Discuss with a partner.

B Read the passage. What possible solutions are mentioned?

▶ 7.8

1   Body image—the way people feel about their appearance—is a big **issue** for many young people today. According to two different studies, more than half the teenage girls in the United States think they should be on a diet, and almost one in five teenage boys are worried about their bodies and their weight.

2   But what's the cause? Many blame the media.[1] Turn on the TV, and you'll likely see beautiful models, handsome actors, and fit sports stars. Open a magazine or newspaper, browse the Internet, and it's unlikely to be any different.

3   Many young people feel pressure[2] to look like these "perfect" people. But for most, this is just not possible. In the United States, for example, the average woman is 163 centimeters tall and weighs 64 kilograms. The average model is 180 centimeters tall and weighs 53 kilograms.

4   When people don't match up to these standards, many develop low **self-esteem**. Some stop eating **properly** in order to lose weight. Others lose so much confidence that they start to **withdraw** from classroom activities at school.

5   Body image issues do not disappear as we get older, either. In the United Kingdom, for example, women over 50 spend more money on cosmetics[3] than any other age group. Older men spend large amounts of money trying to **avoid** hair loss.

6   Is there a solution to the problem? A 2013 study in the United Kingdom recommended that body image lessons be provided in schools. Others believe it's a problem that all of society needs to tackle. As self-esteem advocate Meaghan Ramsey says, "We need to start judging people by what they do, not what they look like."

[1] **the media:** *n.* radio, newspapers, magazines, etc.
[2] **pressure:** *n.* the feeling that you must do something

[3] **cosmetics:** *n.* things that people put on their face and body to look more attractive, e.g., makeup

UNDERSTANDING MAIN IDEAS

What's the main idea of each paragraph? Write the number of each paragraph that contains the main ideas below.

a _____ There is no simple answer. We all need to change the way we think.

b _____ Body image problems also affect adults.

c _____ Many people think they need to look the same as the people in the media.

d __1__ Many young people today are worried about their appearance.

e _____ Some people think the media focuses too much on appearance.

f _____ People can lose confidence if they compare themselves to the people in the media.

UNDERSTANDING STATISTICS

Are the following statements true or false, according to the information in the article? Circle **T** for true or **F** for false.

1 Most teenage girls in the United States believe they should be on a diet.   **T**   **F**

2 More than half of teenage boys in the United States are worried about their weight.   **T**   **F**

3 The average female model in the United States is 17 centimeters taller than the average woman.   **T**   **F**

4 In the United Kingdom, teenage girls spend more money on cosmetics than adults.   **T**   **F**

BUILDING VOCABULARY

A Choose the correct option to complete each sentence.

1 A big **issue** is an important _____ .

  a problem   **b** solution

2 If you have low **self-esteem**, you are _____ in yourself.

  a confident   **b** not confident

3 If you **withdraw** from something, you _____ it.

  a continue to do   **b** stop doing

4 If you do something **properly**, you do it _____ .

  a in a different way   **b** in the correct way

5 If you **avoid** hair loss, you do something to _____ .

  a stop it from happening   **b** make it happen

B **CRITICAL THINKING**

Reflecting Do you think the media affects your **self-esteem**? If so, in what way? What might be some other reasons people have low self-esteem?

> I think the media affects how I feel about my clothing, for sure.

> For me, it's not the media. Other people's opinions have a bigger influence on how I feel.

7D Why thinking you're ugly is bad for you

TEDTALKS

MEAGHAN RAMSEY feels we should **judge** people by what they do, not what they look like. She runs a global program that is helping 17 million young **individuals** improve their self-esteem by encouraging them to **value** their **whole** selves, not just their appearance. Her idea worth spreading is that changing the way we think about beauty can help our health and well-being and can improve society as a whole.

PREVIEWING

Read the paragraph above. Match each **bold** word to its meaning. You will hear these words in the TED Talk.

1 people: _____

2 to think something is important: _____

3 to make an opinion about something: _____

4 all of something: _____

VIEWING

A ▶ **7.9** Watch Part 1 of the TED Talk. Choose the correct answer to each question.

1 Why does Faye dread school?

    a because she doesn't have any friends   **b** because people say that she's ugly

2 Why does Faye post a video of herself online?

    a because her friends do the same thing   **b** so people can comment on her appearance

3 According to Ramsey, why do many others post videos like Faye's?

    a because online comments are really important to them   **b** because they feel alone

B ▶ **7.10** Watch Part 2 of the TED Talk. Circle **T** for true or **F** for false.

1 Body image issues can affect a student's performance at school.   **T**   **F**

2 The problem is worse in the United States than in other countries.   **T**   **F**

3 The main issue is how students think they look, not how they actually look.   **T**   **F**

C ▶ **7.11** Watch Part 3 of the TED Talk. What suggestions does Ramsey make about how to "change our culture's obsession with image"? Check [✓] all that apply.

☐ Think carefully about the pictures and comments that we post on social networks.

☐ Say more nice things about people's appearance to improve their confidence.

☐ Stop letting young people use social networks during school.

☐ Focus less on attractive people and more on those who make a difference in the world.

D CRITICAL THINKING

Applying Read the social media posts below. How do you think Meaghan Ramsey would feel about each one? Discuss with a partner.

"Wow! You lost a lot of weight. Well done!"

"Maria Sharapova is my favorite tennis player. She's so beautiful!"

"Congratulations on your exam result!"

VOCABULARY IN CONTEXT

▶ **7.12** Watch the excerpts from the TED Talk. Choose the correct meaning of the words.

PRESENTATION SKILLS Adding support by giving statistics

> You can use statistics to support any claims you make in a presentation. For example:
>
> **Nine out of ten** people ...   **5 percent** of students ...
> **One in three** women ...   Every day, **500** men ...

A ▶ **7.13** Watch the excerpts from Meaghan Ramsey's TED Talk. Complete the sentences with the numbers you hear.

1 "_____ people every month google, 'Am I ugly?'"

2 "_____ out of _____ girls are now choosing not to do something because they don't think they look good enough."

3 "_____ percent, nearly _____ in _____ teenagers, are withdrawing from classroom debate."

4 "_____ in _____ are not showing up to class at all on days when they don't feel good about it."

B Look again at the statements in **A**. Which of the statistics do you find most surprising? Do you think the numbers would be similar in your country? Discuss with a partner.

7E What do you think?

COMMUNICATE A class poll

A Discuss the questions below with a partner. Explain your answers.

1 Do you think the media in your country focuses too much on appearance?

2 Do you think teenagers worry more than adults about their appearance?

3 Do you think teenage girls have more body issues than boys?

4 Is it OK to comment on a post that asks, "Am I ugly?"?

5 Do you think it's a good idea for schools to have body image lessons?

6 Would you ever consider plastic surgery?

7 Do you worry about the number of "likes" you get on social media?

8 Do you think beauty contests are a bad thing?

B Work as a class. For each question above, take a poll. How many people think "yes"? How many think "no"? Make a note of the results.

> **Declining to answer a question**
> *Sorry, I'd rather not say.*   *I'd prefer not to answer.*   *No comment!*

C Work with a partner. Discuss the results of the class poll. Was anything surprising? Use statistics to describe the results.

> So, 9 out of 20 don't like beauty contests. That's nearly half.

> Yeah. That's surprising! I thought it would be more.

WRITING Describing someone

A What is your best friend like? List four words that describe his or her personality and appearance.

_____   _____   _____   _____

B Use the information in **A** to write a description of your best friend. Does your friend ever worry about his or her appearance?

> My best friend is Alfonso. He's really smart and considerate. He's also really tall and thin. He loves being tall, but he sometimes worries about being too thin ...

8 Wild Places

> **❝** As a filmmaker, I've been from one end of the Earth to the other trying to get the perfect shot. **❞**

Karen Bass
Filmmaker, TED speaker

UNIT GOALS

In this unit, you will …

- talk about natural attractions.
- read about an incredible place.
- watch a TED Talk about the joys of filming the natural world.

WARM UP

▶ **8.1** Watch part of Karen Bass's TED Talk. Answer the questions with a partner.

1 How would you describe the place in the video?
2 Would you like to go there? Why or why not?

Patagonia's Paine massif rises beyond Lake Pehoé, Chile

8A The natural world

VOCABULARY Natural features

A Look at the words in the box below. Which of these things can you see in the picture above? Which of these things do you have in your country? Discuss with a partner.

beach	canyon	desert	island
lake	mountain	ocean	waterfall

B ▶ **8.2** Complete the sentences with words from the box below. One word is extra. Watch and check your answers.

deep	dry	high	long	wide

1 China's Yangtze River is very _____. It flows for 6,300 kilometers.

2 Mont Blanc is a very _____ mountain in Europe. It's 4,809 meters above sea level.

3 Russia's Lake Baikal is extremely _____. Its bottom is 1,285 meters below sea level.

4 In the United States, the Mississippi River is so _____ that you cannot see across it in some places.

C Look back at the words in **A**. Can you name any other examples? Why are they famous? Discuss with a partner.

There's Ninety Mile Beach in Australia. It's really long.

Right, and there's the Grand Canyon in the United States. It's very deep.

LISTENING An amazing place

> **Listening for content words**
> Content words—such as main verbs, nouns, and adjectives—carry the main meaning of a sentence. In spoken English, these words are usually stressed. Focusing on content words can help you understand the speaker's main message.

A ▶ **8.3** Watch the video about Ross Donihue and Marty Schnure's work in Patagonia. What did their work involve? Circle the correct option.

Ross Donihue and Marty Schnure in Patagonia

| studying wildlife | making a map | collecting plants |

B ▶ **8.3** Watch again. Complete the sentences. Circle the correct words.

1 Patagonia is an area shared by (**two** / **three**) countries.

2 Patagonia is usually a very cool and (**wet** / **dry**) place.

3 Donihue's favorite thing about Patagonia is (**the changing conditions** / **the wildlife**).

C CRITICAL THINKING

Personalizing What questions would you like to ask Donihue and Schnure to find out more about their work? Discuss with a partner.

SPEAKING Talking about places

A ▶ **8.4** What is speaker A's favorite island?

A: So where are you going for your vacation this summer?

B: Hawaii. I'm really looking forward to it!   I can't wait / I'm really excited

A: That's great! I know it well.

B: Really? I can't decide which island to visit—Oahu or Maui. I hear that Maui is more relaxing.   quieter / more peaceful

A: Yeah, maybe. But Oahu is more exciting. That's where Honolulu and Waikiki Beach are.

B: So would you say Oahu is the best place in Hawaii?   nicest / most interesting

A: No. Actually, my favorite island is Kauai. It's definitely the most beautiful. It has mountains, canyons, waterfalls, and beaches. I love it there.   prettiest / most scenic

B Practice the conversation with a partner. Practice again using the words on the right.

C List three places in the world you'd like to visit. Explain your ideas to a partner.

_____   _____   _____

I'd love to go to the Grand Canyon. I'd like to hike to the bottom.

Yeah, that sounds great. Me too.

8B The deepest, longest, and most beautiful

LANGUAGE FOCUS Discussing natural wonders

A ▶ **8.5** Read the information. Do you agree with the list?

SEVEN WONDERS of the NATURAL WORLD

Our planet is home to some incredible natural wonders. Here are seven of the most amazing.

The best place to see the **Aurora Borealis** is from northwest Canada.

Mexico's **Copper Canyon** is deeper and longer than the Grand Canyon.

Mount Everest is the highest mountain in the world.

Africa's **Victoria Falls** is the world's largest waterfall.

The Great Barrier Reef is the world's largest coral reef system.

Rio de Janeiro's harbor is one of the most beautiful harbors in the world.

Other volcanoes may be larger than Mexico's **Paricutin Volcano**, but few are more beautiful.

B ▶ **8.6** Two people are talking about the places above. Watch and complete the information.

1 The man thinks Paricutin Volcano is _____ volcano in the world.

2 The woman says Copper Canyon is _____ than the Grand Canyon.

C ▶ **8.7** Watch and study the language in the chart.

Making comparisons	
Comparing two things	**Comparing three or more things**
Copper Canyon is deeper than the Grand Canyon.	The Grand Canyon isn't the deepest canyon in the world.
I think Kauai is more beautiful than Oahu.	I think Kauai is the most beautiful place in Hawaii.
Spring is a better time to visit than summer.	May is the best month to go there.
Is the Amazon longer than the Nile?	Is the Nile the longest river in the world?
No, it isn't.	Yes, it is.
Which is wider—the Nile or the Amazon?	What's the widest river in the world?
The Amazon is (wider).	The Amazon is (the widest).

For more information on **comparative and superlative adjectives**, see Grammar Summary 8 on page 157.

D Complete the sentences. Circle the correct words.

1 Let's go to Sydney in December. The weather is (**better than** / **the best**) in June.

2 Is Canada (**biggest** / **bigger than**) the United States? It's not easy to tell from this map.

3 To me, summer is (**worse than** / **the worst**) time to visit Jeju Island, because of the crowds.

4 I would love to see Iguazu Falls in South America someday. They look (**really** / **more**) beautiful.

5 The Grand Canyon is amazing. But right now it's (**crowded** / **more crowded**) than last year.

6 The Nile is (**long** / **the longest**) river in the world. It can take months to travel from one end to the other.

7 Both the Hawaiian and Galápagos islands sound (**nice** / **the nicest**) to me, but the Galápagos sound (**more interesting** / **the most interesting**).

E ▶ **8.8** Complete the text with the correct form of the words in parentheses. Listen and check your answers.

Mount Fuji is a symbol of Japan. At 3,776 meters, it is
¹_____ (high) mountain in Japan. It is
only 100 kilometers from Tokyo,
²_____ (large) city in the country.

Mount Fuji is one of ³_____ (popular)
tourist attractions in Japan. More than 200,000 people climb
to the top every year. Most visit during the summer months.
Climbing in the summer is ⁴_____ (easy) than
in the winter. Few climb during the winter as the conditions
make it ⁵_____ (dangerous) than usual.

Many people start to climb Mount Fuji at night.
⁶_____ (good) place to experience sunrise is
from the top. Japan, after all, is nicknamed the "Land of the
Rising Sun."

SPEAKING What do you know?

A What do you know about some of the world's most famous natural wonders?
You are going to give each other a quiz. **Student A**: Turn to page 145.
Student B: Turn to page 142.

B Work with a partner. Write three quiz questions of your own. Then ask them to another
pair. (Be sure you know the answers!)

1 _____?

2 _____?

3 _____?

> What's the largest continent in the world?

> Is it Asia?

The Altiplano, or "high plain," of South America is a place of extremes.

8C An otherworldly place

PRE-READING Predicting

A Look at the picture and read the caption. Do you think the statements below are true or false? Discuss with a partner.

1 The Altiplano is a very high place. **T** **F**

2 The Altiplano is in Africa. **T** **F**

3 Very few people live in the Altiplano. **T** **F**

B Skim the article to check your guesses.

▶ **8.9**

In the high Andes of South America lies one of the most incredible **landscapes** in the world. The Altiplano, or "high plain," is a place of extremes.[1] It is the second largest mountain **plateau** in the world. It holds the world's largest high-altitude lake, Lake Titicaca, and the largest salt flat,[2] Salar de Uyuni. At 4,500 meters, it is also higher than many of the world's mountains.

Most of the Altiplano lies within Bolivia and Peru, while its southern parts lie in Chile and Argentina. The Atacama Desert—one of the driest areas on the planet—lies to the southwest. The Amazon rain forest lies to the east.

It is an otherworldly[3] place that looks more like Mars than Earth. High volcanoes **contrast** with deep valleys. Temperatures can change from boiling hot to freezing cold in a single day. Few trees can survive the dry conditions.

But animal life surprisingly thrives[4] here. There are mammals, such as llamas, foxes, and alpacas. There are also birds like the high-flying condors and three **species** of South American flamingos. Millions of people live in the Altiplano, too; most live in the area between Lake Titicaca and Salar de Uyuni. Bolivia's most **populated** city, La Paz, is actually found here.

---

[1] **extremes:** *n.* conditions well beyond the usual
[2] **salt flat:** *n.* an area of flat land covered with a layer of salt
[3] **otherworldly:** *adj.* strange, as if from another planet
[4] **thrive:** *v.* to do well and be successful

UNDERSTANDING MAIN IDEAS

C Read the article. Choose the best alternative title.

    a South America's Natural Wonders   **c** Animals at High Altitude

    b Land of Extremes   **d** The Highest City in the World

UNDERSTANDING DETAILS

A Complete the notes.

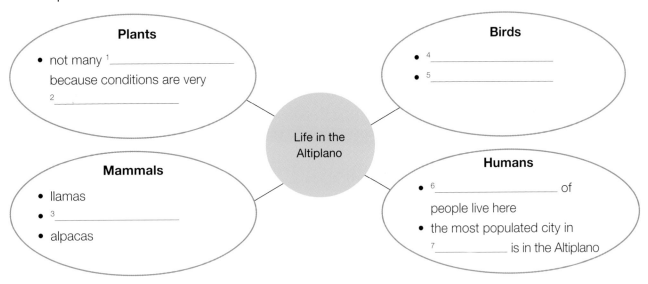

Plants
- not many ¹_____
  because conditions are very
  ²_____

Birds
- ⁴_____
- ⁵_____

Life in the Altiplano

Mammals
- llamas
- ³_____
- alpacas

Humans
- ⁶_____ of people live here
- the most populated city in ⁷_____ is in the Altiplano

B Match each phrase to the place in the article that it describes.

    1 La Paz   ○   ○ the largest high-altitude lake in the world

    2 The Atacama Desert   ○   ○ the largest salt flat in the world

    3 Lake Titicaca   ○   ○ one of the driest areas in the world

    4 Salar de Uyuni   ○   ○ the most populated city in the Altiplano

BUILDING VOCABULARY

A Complete the definitions below with a word in blue from the passage.

    1 A _____ is a large area of high, flat land.

    2 A _____ is everything you see when you look at an area of land.

    3 A _____ is a group of animals or plants with the same characteristics.

B Choose the correct option to complete the definitions below.

    1 If a place is **populated**, people (**live** / **don't live**) there.

    2 If two things **contrast**, they are (**the same** / **different**).

C **CRITICAL THINKING**

Personalizing Are there any incredible **landscapes** in your country? What kinds of animal **species** live there? Discuss with a partner.

8D Unseen footage, untamed nature

TEDTALKS

KAREN BASS's idea worth spreading is that world travel and new technology have allowed her to see and **capture** on film some **wonderful** things in nature. Bass shows that when you have a job you love, even long hours and **tough**, challenging situations can't affect your passion for your work.

PREVIEWING

Read the paragraph above. Circle the correct option for each sentence below. You will hear these words in the TED Talk.

1 If you **capture** something on film, you (**record** / **erase**) it.

2 Something that is **wonderful** is (**great** / **sad**).

3 A **tough** job is very (**easy** / **difficult**).

VIEWING

A ▶ **8.10** Watch Part 1 of the TED Talk. Complete the sentences. Choose the correct option.

1 Bass believes she's "lucky" in her job because she _____ .

    a has a passion for using new technology   **b** can share her work with millions of people

2 The latest technology helps her to _____ .

    a get new images of animals that people have never seen before   **b** work together with people all around the world

3 Bass says she is also excited when _____ .

    a she travels to a place no one has been before   **b** new animal species are discovered

B ▶ **8.11** Watch Part 2 of the TED Talk. Which of the diagrams below shows the length of a bat's tongue if the bat were the size of a human?

a

b

c

C ▶ **8.12** Watch Part 3 of the TED Talk. Choose the correct option.

1 Why did Bass first go to the Altiplano?

    a to backpack   **b** to live   **c** to film animals

2 What does Bass say is an advantage of the Altiplano's thin atmosphere?

    a Unique animals live there.   **b** It almost never rains.   **c** It's easy to see stars.

D CRITICAL THINKING

Applying **Imagine you are a filmmaker like Karen Bass. Which place would you like to visit? What would you like to film? Discuss with a partner.**

VOCABULARY IN CONTEXT

▶ **8.13** Watch the excerpts from the TED Talk. Choose the correct meaning of the words.

PRESENTATION SKILLS Showing enthusiasm

You can show you are enthusiastic through the kind of language you use. For example, instead of using words like *good* or *nice*, you can use stronger adjectives such as:

amazing   *brilliant*   *fantastic*   *magnificent*   *wonderful*

A ▶ **8.14** Watch the excerpts from Karen Bass's TED Talk. Complete the sentences below with the words you hear.

1 "There are so many _____ places. But some locations draw you back time and time again."

2 "But the advantage of that _____ thin atmosphere is that it enables you to see the stars in the heavens with _____ clarity."

3 "Thank you so much for letting me share some images of our _____, _____ Earth."

B Read the excerpt from a presentation below. What words could you add to make the speaker sound more enthusiastic?

India is my favorite place in the world. There are so many things you can do there. You can visit the beaches in Goa, sail down the River Ganges, and of course, no trip to this place is complete without seeing the Taj Mahal.

C Work with a partner. Take turns reading the script above. Include some strong adjectives to help you sound enthusiastic.

The Parinacota volcano, high in the Altiplano

8E Our natural wonders

COMMUNICATE A tourism poster

A Work in a group. Imagine you are part of your country's tourism board. Brainstorm a list of your country's natural attractions. Think about lakes, rivers, forests, parks, etc.

> We have some nice national parks. How about one of those?

> Good idea. I think Seacoast Park is the most famous park.

B Which attractions would foreign visitors like the most? Agree on three.

Expressing agreement

I agree.   *You're right.*   *That's a good point.*   *I couldn't agree more.*

C Create a poster for your attractions. Think about what you want to include and take notes. Include visuals or other things to make it interesting.

best time to visit	**what's special about it**	**interesting facts**
how to get there	**what to see there**	**what to do there**

D Hold a class poster session. Look at your classmates' posters and present your own. Remember to sound enthusiastic when you present.

WRITING A place I'd like to visit

A Take notes on a place you'd like to visit.

Place: _____

Location: _____

Best time to go: _____

Why I want to visit: _____

B Write about the place. Make it sound as interesting as possible.

> I'd like to visit Whistler Mountain in British Columbia, Canada. You can visit any time, but for me the best time to visit is the winter. I love to ski, and Whistler has really amazing skiing.

9 Achievements

> **“** Beneath our feet: 90 percent of all the world's ice, 70 percent of all the world's freshwater. **”**

Robert Swan
Polar explorer, TED Speaker

UNIT GOALS

In this unit, you will ...

- talk about personal achievements.
- read about an extreme explorer.
- watch a TED Talk about protecting a special place.

WARM UP

▶ **9.1** Watch part of Robert Swan's TED Talk. Answer the questions with a partner.

1 Where do you think the speaker is?

2 Why do you think he's there?

Climbers celebrate reaching the top of a mountain in Antarctica.

9A We did it!

VOCABULARY Personal achievements

A Match the words in each set.

1	run	○	○ into shape 2	7	win	○	○ a job 9
2	get	○	○ a new language 3	8	pass	○	○ a competition 7
3	learn	○	○ a marathon 1	9	get	○	○ an exam 8

4	climb	○	○ college 6	10	get	○	○ a presentation 10
5	win	○	○ a mountain 4	11	give	○	○ into college 10
6	finish	○	○ an award 5	12	start	○	○ a business 12

B Which of the achievements above do you think are the most difficult? Why? Discuss with a partner.

> I think running a marathon is the most difficult.

> Really? I think learning a new language is more difficult.

LISTENING My great achievement

Scott Leefe taking part in a marathon in Iceland

> **Listening for past time expressions**
> Listening for certain time expressions helps you understand when the speaker is talking about the past. For example:
>
> one year **ago**   **last** week   **When I was a child,** ...

A ▶ **9.2** Scott Leefe is an amateur marathon runner. Watch and check [✓] his achievement.

☐ He ran 12 marathons in one year.

☐ He broke a national record for the marathon.

☐ He won a marathon in Iceland.

B ▶ **9.2** Watch again. Match the events to the places.

1 Leefe ran his first marathon in   ○   ○ Reykjavik, Iceland.

2 His favorite marathon was in   ○   ○ Okinawa, Japan.

3 His most difficult race was in   ○   ○ Gwacheon, Korea.

4 He finished in third place in   ○   ○ Kuala Lumpur, Malaysia.

C CRITICAL THINKING

Personalizing Do you know anyone who achieved something similar to Leefe? Discuss with a partner.

SPEAKING Talking about an achievement

A ▶ **9.3** What was speaker B's achievement?

A: How was the race last week?   speech contest / talent show

B: Pretty good. I got second place.   came in second / was runner-up

A: Oh, well done!   congratulations / good job

B: Thanks! It wasn't easy.

A: Did you get a prize?

B: Yeah, I did. I won a $50 book voucher.

A: Great! You must be really happy.   really pleased / delighted

B: I am. It was really hard work, but it was worth it.

B Practice the conversation with a partner. Practice again using the words on the right.

C Think of something you achieved. Choose one of these ideas or think of your own. Join a group and talk about your achievement.

a time you won something	a time you achieved a goal
a time you learned something	a time you passed an important exam

9B Exploring the world

LANGUAGE FOCUS Discussing past events

A ▶ 9.4 Read the information. Which achievement do you think is the most interesting?

MILESTONES IN EXPLORATION

Edmund Hillary and Tenzing Norgay climbed Mount Everest.
1953

Neil Armstrong and Buzz Aldrin became the first people to walk on the moon.
1969

Robert Swan walked to the South Pole.
1986

Ann Bancroft and Liv Arnesen traveled across Antarctica.
2001

Gennady Padalka broke the record for the longest time spent in space.
2015

1963
Valentina Tereshkova became the first woman to travel to space.

1985
Robert Ballard discovered the *Titanic*.

1999
Bertrand Piccard and Brian Jones flew a balloon nonstop around the world.

2010
Sixteen-year-old Jessica Watson sailed alone around the world.

B ▶ 9.5 Listen to more information about Ann Bancroft and Liv Arnesen's achievement. Complete the sentences.

1 Before they became explorers, Ann Bancroft and Liv Arnesen worked as _____.

2 In 2001, they became the first women to cross the Antarctic on _____.

3 Their journey across Antarctica took _____ months.

C ▶ 9.6 Watch and study the language in the chart.

Talking about the past
In 1969, Apollo 11's Lunar Module landed on the moon.
Neil Armstrong was the first to walk on the moon. Buzz Aldrin was second.
They were on the surface of the moon for just over two hours.
Michael Collins was also on the mission but he didn't walk on the moon.
Piccard and Jones began their balloon flight around the world in 1999.

Were they successful?	Yes, they were.
Did they make any stops on their journey?	No, they didn't.
How long did the journey take?	It took almost 20 days.

For more information on **simple past**, see Grammar Summary 9 on page 157.

D Look back at the infographic. Write short answers to the following questions.

1 Was Valentina Tereshkova the first woman in space? _Yes, she was._

2 Did Ann Bancroft and Liv Arnesen journey across the Arctic? _Yes they didn't_

3 Did Edmund Hillary discover the *Titanic*? _No he didn't_

4 Did Robert Swan walk to the South Pole? _yes he did_

5 Were Piccard and Jones the first people to walk on the moon? _No they werent_

E ▶ **9.7** Complete the information with the correct form of the words in parentheses. Listen and check your answers.

Sarah McNair-Landry [1]_____grew up_____ (grow up) in northern Canada. Her parents were Arctic guides, so it's not surprising that she [2]____wanted____ (want) to explore from an early age. At age 18, she [3]____skied____ (ski) to the South Pole. She [4]____was____ (be) the youngest person ever to do this.

In 2007, McNair-Landry, her brother, and a friend [5]____decided____ (decide) to snow-kite 2,300 kilometers across Greenland. She [6]____wanted____ (want) to raise awareness of global warming, and she [7]____hoped____ (hope) to inspire a new generation of explorers.

In 2015, she and a friend [8]____traveled____ (travel) for 120 days in the Arctic by dogsled. According to McNair-Landry, the most difficult thing about the trip [9]____was____ (be) keeping the dogs happy. Often they simply [10]____didn't want____ (not want) to run.

Sarah McNair-Landry and her dogsled in the Arctic

F Use the words to write questions. Ask and answer them with a partner.

1 you / pass / your last exam? _Did you pass your last exam?_

2 when / you / last win / a prize? _when did you last win a prize?_

3 what / you / achieve / last year? _what did you achieve last year_

4 be / you / a good student / in middle school? _were you a good student in middle shcool_

SPEAKING Round-the-world adventure

A Read the beginning of the story of Jessica Watson's round-the-world sailing trip.

Australian Jessica Watson sailed around the world alone. She left Sydney on October 18, 2009. She was just 16 years old.

B You are going to read more about Jessica Watson's trip. **Student A:** Turn to page 144. **Student B:** Turn to page 141.

1 yes he did
2 10 moths ago
3 traveled usa

4 Yes she was

A photo of Robert Swan and a team member taken during the Antarctica expedition, 1985

9C Extreme survival

PRE-READING Scanning

A Scan the passage quickly. What was Robert Swan's great achievement?

B Read the passage to check your answer.

▶ 9.8

1 At age 11, Robert Swan knew he wanted to be an adventurer. Inspired by famous polar explorers Roald Amundsen and Robert Scott, Swan wanted to become the first person to walk to both the North and South Poles. People told him he was crazy, but in 1985, after years of raising money, the first part of this adventure could begin.

2 In January 1986, Swan and his team arrived at the South Pole following a 1,400-kilometer journey through Antarctica's **intense** conditions. Just three years later, Swan put together a new team to **head** to the North Pole. After walking 1,000 kilometers in 60 days, the team arrived at its destination.[1] Swan, in his own words, became "the first person stupid enough to walk to both Poles."

3 During those two expeditions,[2] however, Swan noticed some **frightening** things. At the South Pole, his eyes changed color and his skin blistered[3] due to a hole in the ozone layer.[4] At the North Pole, 1,000 kilometers from safety, the ice started to melt **beneath** his feet. This was four months earlier than the usual "melt season." These experiences made Swan realize something—the Poles were in real danger.

4 That feeling never left Swan. He now works to raise awareness about climate change and the ice **melt** of the South and North Poles. In doing this, Swan hopes that he can not only help in the preservation of these two amazing places, but also in our own **survival** here on Earth.

[1] **destination:** *n.* the place you're going to
[2] **expedition:** *n.* an organized trip for a special purpose
[3] **blister:** *v.* to develop painful swelling on the skin
[4] **the ozone layer:** the part of Earth's atmosphere that protects us from the sun's ultraviolet rays

UNDERSTANDING MAIN IDEAS

Circle the main idea for each paragraph number below.

1 a From a young age, Swan wanted to explore the North and South Poles.

  b Swan was the youngest man to walk to the South Pole.

2 a The journey to the North Pole was more dangerous than the one to the South Pole.

  b In the 1980s, Swan became the first person to walk to both Poles.

3 a During the expeditions, Swan saw that the Poles were in danger.

  b Swan thought about stopping the expeditions due to the many dangers.

4 a Swan hopes that one day he can return to the South Pole.

  b These days, Swan works to teach people about the dangers of climate change.

UNDERSTANDING DETAILS

Complete the Venn diagram using the information below.

a 1,000-kilometer journey

b 1,400-kilometer journey

c traveled with a team

d arrived at destination in 1986

e arrived at destination in 1989

f ice started to melt four months earlier than usual

g skin and eyes damaged due to hole in ozone layer

Swan's expedition to the South Pole

Swan's expedition to the North Pole

BUILDING VOCABULARY

A Complete the paragraph below using the correct form of words in blue from the passage.

More than 100 years ago, Robert Falcon Scott [1]_____ to Antarctica in an attempt to become the first person to reach the South Pole. In January 1912, after a long and difficult expedition in the [2]_____ cold, Scott and his team successfully reached their destination. However, when they got there, they found that a Norwegian team, led by Roald Amundsen, had already arrived 34 days earlier. On the return journey, Scott's team faced a [3]_____ struggle for [4]_____ as they suffered in the extreme conditions. Sadly, Scott and his four companions all died before they reached home.

B Complete the definitions below. Circle the correct words.

  1 If something is **beneath** you, it is (**above** / **below**) you.

  2 An example of something that can **melt** is (**ice cream** / **orange juice**).

C CRITICAL THINKING

Applying What other places in the world have **intense** conditions? Discuss with a partner.

9D Let's save the last pristine continent

TEDTALKS

ROBERT SWAN has made it his **mission** to protect Antarctica. He knows from experience that what is happening there **threatens** the Earth's long-term health. His idea worth spreading is that the **preservation** of Antarctica is **linked** to our survival, and that it's within our power to slow down the melting of ice in the South Pole.

PREVIEWING

Read the paragraph above. Match each **bold** word to its meaning. You will hear these words in the TED Talk.

1 connected: _____

2 a very important task: _____

3 to put in danger: _____

4 keeping the same: _____

VIEWING

A ▶ 9.9 Watch Part 1 of the TED Talk. Circle **T** for true or **F** for false.

1 Swan describes himself as an environmentalist.   **T**   **F**

2 On the expedition, Swan's team had radios so that they could call for help. **T**   **F**

3 It was so cold that water could freeze in their eyes.   **T**   **F**

4 The journey to the South Pole took 90 days.   **T**   **F**

B ▶ 9.10 Watch Part 2 of the TED Talk. Complete the summary with the numbers you hear.

Robert Swan has taken more than [1]_____ businesspeople and students to Antarctica so that they could experience the place for themselves. During these visits, they removed [2]_____ tons of old waste metal over a period of [3]_____ years and recycled it in South America. Swan has been to Antarctica [4]_____ times. He believes everyone who goes there returns home as a champion[1] for this amazing place.

[1] **champion:** *n.* a supporter or defender of something

C ▶ 9.11 Watch Part 3 of the TED Talk. What "simple solution" does Swan suggest to stop the melting of Antarctica's ice? Circle the correct answer.

a We should all use more renewable energy. If we do, people won't need to use Antarctica's resources and we can also slow down the melting of Antarctica's ice.

b Antarctica can provide a lot of renewable energy. If we use energy from Antarctica, people will realize how special the place is. It can also help slow down global warming.

D CRITICAL THINKING

Inferring Discuss the following questions with a partner.

1 Why do you think Robert Swan chose to have no backup on his expedition to the South Pole?

2 Robert Swan describes India and China as "game-changing nations." What do you think he means?

VOCABULARY IN CONTEXT

▶ **9.12** Watch the excerpts from the TED Talk. Choose the correct meaning of the words.

PRESENTATION SKILLS Pausing effectively

Pausing at an appropriate time allows the audience time to stop and consider the speaker's message. You can pause after an important point or a question you want the audience to think about.

A ▶ **9.13** Watch the excerpt. Notice how Swan uses pauses when he speaks.

B ▶ **9.14** Read the excerpt below. Mark with a **/** where you think Swan will pause. Watch and check your guesses.

I have faced head-on these places, and to walk across a melting ocean of ice is without doubt the most frightening thing that's ever happened to me.

C Look at the paragraph about Robert Swan on page 104. Imagine this is part of a presentation you are giving. Mark with a **/** where you think you should pause. Then practice reading the paragraph to your partner.

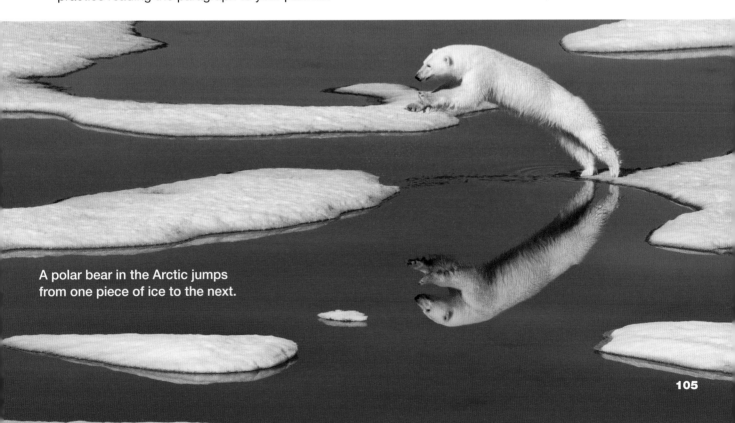

A polar bear in the Arctic jumps from one piece of ice to the next.

COMMUNICATE An achievement

A Work with a partner. Think of a person who made an important achievement in one of the following categories.

sports	medicine	education	exploration
entertainment	inventions	science	technology

B Research information about this person. Find answers to some of the following questions. Take notes.

What does this person do?

Why did you choose this person?

What was his or her achievement?

What did he or she need to do to achieve it?

What's your opinion of this person's achievement?

Did anyone help him or her?

Why is the achievement important?

What other events in this person's life are important?

How long did it take?

C Use your notes to prepare to talk about the person and his or her achievement. Then tell another pair. Answer any questions.

> **Interrupting politely**
>
> *Sorry, can I just stop you there?*
>
> *Sorry, do you mind if I ask a question?*
>
> *Sorry, can I just ask something?*

WRITING A biography

Use your notes from the activity above to write about a person who achieved something important in his or her life. Include information about the person's background and childhood.

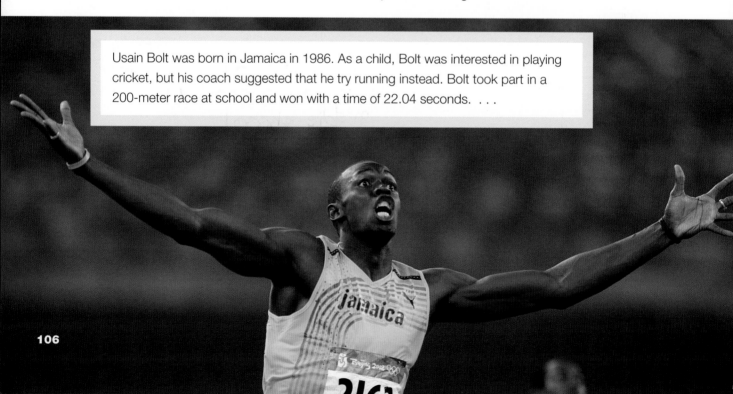

Usain Bolt was born in Jamaica in 1986. As a child, Bolt was interested in playing cricket, but his coach suggested that he try running instead. Bolt took part in a 200-meter race at school and won with a time of 22.04 seconds. . . .

Presentation 3

MODEL PRESENTATION

A Complete the transcript of the presentation using the words in the box.

ago	beach	best	didn't	in	largest
most	quite	stayed	too	was	were

I'd like to talk to you about the ¹_____ amazing place I've ever visited.

The Great Barrier Reef is the ²_____ coral reef system

³_____ the world. It stretches for more than 2,300 kilometers off

the east coast of Australia. You can even see it from space! I went there with my

best friend about two years ⁴_____. We both really love diving,

so this ⁵_____ our dream holiday. We ⁶_____

in a hotel on Heron Island, which is just off the coast. It's a beautiful

place. The ⁷_____ thing about the island was that we

⁸_____ need to take a boat to visit the reef—the reef was

right there, just off the ⁹_____.

We saw some amazing things while we were diving. There

¹⁰_____ so many different kinds of colorful fish. We even saw a sea

snake that swam very close to us. To be honest, I was ¹¹_____ scared!

The only bad thing about my trip was that it was much ¹²_____ short. We

stayed for three days and spent most of our time in the water. I'd love to go back again

and maybe go diving in a different place.

Thanks for listening.

B ▶ **P.3** Watch the presentation and check your answers.

C ▶ **P.3** Review the list of presentation skills from Units 1–9 below. Which does the
speaker use? Check [✓] each skill used as you watch again.

The speaker …
- introduces herself ☐
- uses effective body language ☐
- introduces her topic ☐
- uses effective hand gestures ☐
- involves the audience ☐
- gives some statistics ☐
- shows enthusiasm ☐
- pauses effectively ☐
- thanks the audience ☐

YOUR TURN

A You are going to plan and give a short presentation to a partner about a place you've visited, or a place you'd like to visit. Use some or all of the questions below to make some notes.

What's the name of the place?

Where is it exactly?

What's special about it?

What did you do there? / What would you like to do there?

B Look at the useful phrases in the box below. Think about which ones you will need in your presentation.

> **Useful phrases**
>
> | | |
> |---|---|
> | Natural features: | beach, canyon, desert, island, lake, landscape, mountain, ocean, waterfall |
> | Adjectives to describe natural features: | deep, dry, high, long, wide |
> | Stronger adjectives: | amazing, brilliant, fantastic, magnificent, wonderful |
> | Past time expressions: | ago, last, When I was … |

C Work with a partner. Take turns giving your presentation using your notes. Use some of the presentation skills from Units 1–9. As you listen, check [✓] each skill your partner uses.

The speaker …
- introduces himself / herself ☐
- uses effective body language ☐
- introduces his or her topic ☐
- uses effective hand gestures ☐
- involves the audience ☐
- gives some statistics ☐
- shows enthusiasm ☐
- pauses effectively ☐
- thanks the audience ☐

D Give your partner some feedback on their talk. Include two things you liked, and one thing he or she can improve.

> That was great. You paused effectively, and you showed enthusiasm. But you forgot to introduce your topic.

10 Creative Cities

> **"** It was dirt. It was nothing. It was nowhere. And so we just started imagining, what else could happen in this building? **"**

Theaster Gates
Social activist, TED speaker

DOWNTOWN CHICAGO

UNIVERSITY OF CHICAGO

SOUTH SIDE CH

UNIT GOALS

In this unit, you will ...

- describe neighborhoods.
- read about someone who is using art to improve neighborhoods.
- watch a TED Talk about making positive changes in a neighborhood.

WARM UP

▶ **10.1** Watch part of Theaster Gates's TED Talk. Answer the questions with a partner.

1 What do you think Gates did with the building?
2 Does your neighborhood have many empty old buildings? Why or why not?

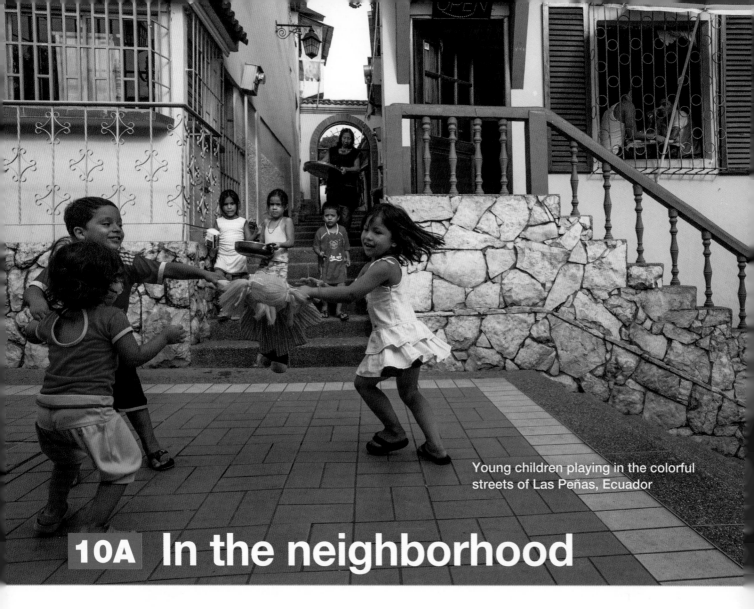

Young children playing in the colorful streets of Las Peñas, Ecuador

10A In the neighborhood

VOCABULARY Qualities of a neighborhood

A Match the words in each set.

1 clean	○ — ○	traffic	**5** low	○ ○	buildings
2 affordable	○ ⟍ ○	streets	**6** green	○ ○	crime rate
3 heavy	○ ○	housing	**7** reliable	○ ○	space
4 friendly	○ ○	neighbors	**8** vacant	○ ○	public transportation

B Which of the phrases above describe positive qualities of a neighborhood? Which describe negative qualities? Compare with a partner. Are there any you disagree on?

C Work with a partner. What are some other qualities of a good neighborhood? A bad neighborhood?

> I think a good neighborhood needs a lot of stores nearby.

> I agree. And there need to be nice places for young people to hang out.

LISTENING The neighborhood where I grew up

> **Identifying pros and cons**
> Taking notes using a chart can help you understand the pros
> (good points) and cons (bad points) of something.

A ▶ **10.2** Craig Albrightson is talking about his hometown in South Africa.
Watch and circle the topics he mentions.

green space	crime	housing	traffic
nightlife	public transportation	neighbors	jobs

B ▶ **10.2** Watch again. Complete the chart with words from **A**.
Add any extra details you hear.

Pros	Cons

Craig Albrightson,
Pietermaritzburg

C CRITICAL THINKING

Evaluating Does Albrightson generally like or dislike his neighborhood?

SPEAKING Talking about your neighborhood

A ▶ **10.3** What doesn't speaker B like about her new neighborhood?

A: I hear you moved to a new place.   apartment / house

B: Yeah, I did. I moved last month.

A: So how do you like your neighborhood?

B: Well, it's OK. The streets are really clean and there are
a lot of parks nearby, but the traffic is really heavy.   stores / restaurants

A: Yeah? Maybe you should take the train.

B: I thought about it, but I heard it's not very reliable.

A: So why don't you buy a bike? It's good exercise.   how about buying / why not buy

B: Yeah, that's a good idea. I'll think about it.   not a bad idea / a great idea

B Practice the conversation with a partner. Practice again using the words on the right.

C Think about your neighborhood. What are its pros and cons? Write notes in the chart.
Work with a partner. Share what you like and don't like about your neighborhood.

Pros	Cons

10B Nice neighborhoods

LANGUAGE FOCUS Giving advice and making suggestions

A ▶ **10.4** Read the information. Which things describe your neighborhood?

WHAT MAKES A GREAT NEIGHBORHOOD?

What do people look for when choosing a neighborhood? A recent survey found that personal safety tops the list, but many other things also help.

1 SAFETY AND LOW CRIME
2 GREEN SPACE AND PARKS
4 AIR QUALITY
7 GOOD ROADS
8 GOOD SCHOOLS
3 AVAILABILITY OF JOBS
6 WATER QUALITY
5 ENTERTAINMENT AND NIGHTLIFE

B ▶ **10.5** A couple are talking about where to move. Watch and check [✓] the neighborhoods that each person likes.

	Brentwood	Crestview	Woodlands
The man			
The woman			

C ▶ **10.6** Watch and study the language in the chart.

Offering suggestions	
Let's Maybe (we/you) can (We/You) could One thing (we/you) could do is	move to a new neighborhood.
Why don't (we/you) move to a new neighborhood?	
How about moving to a new neighborhood?	
What should (I/we) do?	We/You should live in Crestview. We/You shouldn't move to Woodlands.

For more information on **should** and **shouldn't**, see Grammar Summary 10 on page 158.

D Match the sentence parts to make suggestions.

1 You should   ○   ○   walk alone at night. It's not safe.

2 Why don't you   ○   ○   check out the local nightlife together sometime.

3 How about   ○   ○   get a bike and use the bike lanes?

4 You shouldn't   ○   ○   planting some flowers to make your yard prettier?

5 Let's   ○   ○   use public transportation so that you can save money.

E ▶ **10.7** Circle the correct words in the conversation. Listen and check your answers.

A: I really like living in Ottawa, but I don't like where we live now.

B: I know what you mean. Well, how about [1](**find** / **finding**) a new neighborhood?

A: Yeah. We could [2](**move** / **moving**) downtown. The shopping is great there.

B: Yeah, but housing isn't very affordable. Maybe we could [3](**move** / **moving**) near the Greenbelt.

A: That's not a bad idea. I have a few friends in that area.

B: Great. Why don't you [4](**ask** / **asking**) them what it's like?

The Greenbelt surrounding Ottawa's downtown area

F Complete each suggestion with your own ideas.

1 A: I want to live in a fun, exciting part of the city.

 B: You should _____ .

2 A: I'd love to move to an area with a lot of green space.

 B: Maybe you could _____ .

3 A: I want to find a cheap apartment downtown as quickly as possible.

 B: Why don't you _____ ?

SPEAKING The right neighborhood

A Read the descriptions below. Three people are moving to your city and are looking for a suitable neighborhood.

John	Makiko	Miguel
"I'm a student, and I'd like a quiet neighborhood with affordable housing. I want to live near the university. It would be nice to have some green space or a park nearby."	"I just started a job in the city, so I'd like to live in a fun neighborhood close to downtown with good public transportation. I want to be close to nice cafés and restaurants."	"I'm an artist and would like to live in an older part of the city. I'd love to find a place with huge rooms for my studio. I don't have much money, so it needs to be affordable."

B Work with a partner. Recommend a neighborhood in your city that would be suitable for each of the people above. Give reasons for your recommendations.

I think John should live in Rochworth. It's quiet, cheap, and near the university.

Good idea. Or maybe he could live in Whitdale. There are a lot of parks.

Theaster Gates's first art project in the UK saw nonstop musical performances held in the ruins of an old church.

10C Reshaping a city

PRE-READING Previewing

Read the first paragraph. What problems on the South Side of Chicago are mentioned? Discuss with a partner.

▶ 10.8

1 The South Side of Chicago is a part of the city that has seen better days. Crime is a problem, and there are few jobs. Many **blocks** contain vacant buildings. But one **resident** is using his art to bring new life to the place.

2 Theaster Gates saw the **decline** of his neighborhood firsthand. As he grew up, he watched as buildings were demolished[1] by the local government or abandoned[2] by their owners. But as a potter,[3] Gates knew how to make beautiful things from very little. In 2008, he decided to buy a vacant house not far from his own home, and he started to **renovate** it.

3 He used the house to **stage** exhibitions[4] and meetings, and the site soon attracted many visitors. The success of the project led Gates to buy more properties—turning them into cultural centers and meeting places. As Gates says, "We were slowly starting to reshape how people imagined the South Side of the city."

4 One building, named Listening House, has a collection of old books that were donated by publishing companies[5] and bookstores. Another building was turned into a movie theater and named Black Cinema House. It became so popular that soon there wasn't enough room for all the visitors and a new **location** needed to be found.

5 Gates is now a well-known international artist. He has taken part in art shows in Germany and the United Kingdom, and in 2014, he was named as one of the most powerful people in contemporary art[6] by *Art Review* magazine. But Gates hasn't forgotten his neighborhood, and his work in Chicago continues. Gates has helped design a million-dollar art project for one of the South Side's subway stations.

[1] **demolish:** *v.* to completely destroy something
[2] **abandon:** *v.* to leave something
[3] **potter:** *n.* a person who makes pots, dishes, etc., from clay
[4] **exhibition:** *n.* an event in which art is shown to the public
[5] **publishing companies:** *n.* companies that make books
[6] **contemporary art:** *n.* art made by artists in the modern period

UNDERSTANDING PURPOSE

Read the passage. Match each paragraph with its purpose.

Paragraph 1   ○   ○   explains why Gates started his first renovation project.

Paragraph 2   ○   ○   describes how Gates's first project led to more.

Paragraph 3   ○   ○   introduces and describes Chicago's South Side.

Paragraph 4   ○   ○   gives examples of two of Gates's projects in Chicago.

Paragraph 5   ○   ○   describes how Gates continues to work in Chicago despite international fame.

UNDERSTANDING DETAILS

Are the following statements true, false, or not given according to the passage?
Circle **T** for true, **F** for false, or **NG** for not given.

1 Theaster Gates grew up in Chicago.	T	F	NG
2 The first house Gates renovated was near his home.	T	F	NG
3 Listening House is much bigger than Black Cinema House.	T	F	NG
4 Few people visited Black Cinema House.	T	F	NG
5 Gates has had art shows in Europe.	T	F	NG
6 Gates continues to work in Chicago.	T	F	NG

BUILDING VOCABULARY

A Match the words in **blue** from the passage to their definitions.

1 block   ○   ○   to produce a play, performance, musical, etc.

2 resident   ○   ○   to make repairs to improve a place's condition

3 renovate   ○   ○   someone who lives in a particular place

4 stage   ○   ○   an area of land with streets on all its sides

5 location   ○   ○   a decrease in quality or importance

6 decline   ○   ○   a place where something happens

B CRITICAL THINKING

Applying In what other ways could you **renovate**
a vacant building to create community gatherings?
Discuss with a partner.

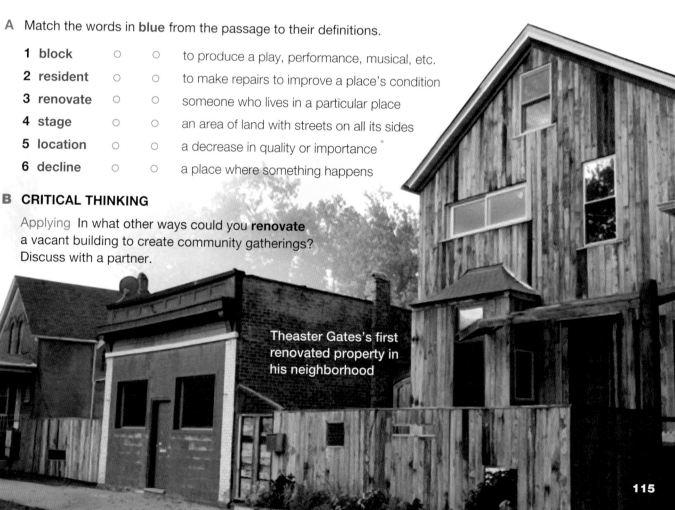

Theaster Gates's first renovated property in his neighborhood

10D How to revive a neighborhood

TEDTALKS

Theaster Gates decided to **tackle** his Chicago neighborhood's problems by **reshaping** and reimagining **abandoned** buildings. His idea worth spreading is that art can be a force for social change, bringing new life to buildings, neighborhoods, and entire cities.

PREVIEWING

Read the paragraph above. Choose the correct meaning of each **bold** word. You will hear these words in the TED Talk.

1 When you **tackle** a problem, you (**ignore** / **deal with**) it.

2 To **reshape** something means to (**make a copy** / **change the structure**) of it.

3 An **abandoned** building is one that the owner (**left** / **just bought**).

VIEWING

A ▶ **10.9** Watch Part 1 of the TED Talk. What problem in his neighborhood does Gates talk about?

   a high crime   **b** vacant buildings   **c** not many jobs

B ▶ **10.10** Watch Part 2 of the TED Talk. Put the events in the order they happened. One option is extra.

   a Gates renovated the building.   **d** Gates began to sweep as a kind of performance art.

   b Gates bought other buildings.   **e** People started to come to Gates's building.

   c Gates got a new job to earn money.   **f** Gates used the building to stage exhibitions.

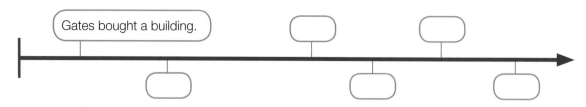

Gates bought a building.

C ▶ **10.11** Watch Part 3 of the TED Talk. Circle the correct option to complete each sentence.

1 The Arts Bank project was difficult to finance because
(**no one was interested in the neighborhood** / **the costs were very high**).

2 The Arts Bank is now used as a
(**free school for adults** / **place for exhibitions and performances**).

3 Gates is now (**giving advice to others** / **doing art exhibitions**) around the country.

D CRITICAL THINKING

Interpreting Look at the diagram from Gates's TED Talk. What does it show? Choose the correct option.

a how Gates's project faced difficulties

b how Gates's project grew in size

c how news about Gates's block spread

CITY

NEIGHBORHOOD

COUNTRY

WORLD

VOCABULARY IN CONTEXT

▶ **10.12** Watch the excerpts from the TED Talk. Choose the correct meaning of the words.

PRESENTATION SKILLS Paraphrasing key points

> When giving a presentation, speakers often paraphrase their key points to make sure their audience understands. When you paraphrase, you repeat the same point but use different words.

A ▶ **10.13** Watch part of Theaster Gates's TED Talk. Complete the sentence with the words you hear. Notice how Gates paraphrases his key point.

"In some ways, it feels very much like I'm a potter, that we tackle the things that are at

our wheel, we _____ with the _____ that we have to think about this next bowl that I want

to make."

B Match the phrases below to make sentences from Gates's TED Talk.
▶ **10.14** Watch the excerpt to check your answers.

1 "It was dirt. It was nothing.   ○   ○ **a** how to start with the things that are in front of you."

2 "We tricked it out.   ○   ○ **b** It was nowhere."

3 "We brought some heat,   ○   ○ **c** We made it as beautiful as we could."

4 "how to start with what you got,   ○   ○ **d** ... we kind of made a fire."

C Write a sentence to paraphrase each of the points below. Compare your ideas with a partner.

1 The most important thing about a neighborhood is safety.

_____

2 My neighborhood is really green.

_____

A mural painted on the side of the Cultural Museum in Santa Fe, United States

10E A better neighborhood

COMMUNICATE Planning neighborhood improvements

A A city has some problems in one of its neighborhoods, and many of the residents are unhappy. You have been asked by the local government to plan some changes to solve the problems. Turn to page 146, look at the map, and read about the problems.

B Work in a group. Brainstorm ideas together and choose the best suggestions to make a plan. Sketch the changes you want to make on the map.

> OK. I think we should build a park somewhere.

> Good idea. How about here, near the river?

C Work with a member from another group. Explain the changes that your group wants to make. Did you have any different ideas?

Describing steps		
First, ... / Firstly, ...	*Second, ... / Secondly, ...*	*Third, ... / Thirdly, ...*

WRITING Creative suggestions

Imagine your town or city wants to renovate a large old building downtown. The local government has set up a website to ask the community to suggest creative ideas for how to use the building. Write some suggestions to post on the website.

> I have a good idea for how to use the building. We could turn it into an eco-aquarium. We could include endangered species from around the world and power the whole place with solar energy ...

11 Picture Perfect

" I'm here to share my photography. Or is it photography? "

Erik Johansson
Photographer, TED speaker

UNIT GOALS

In this unit, you will …

- talk about and describe photographs.
- read about some incredible photographs.
- watch a TED Talk about a different kind of photography.

WARM UP

▶ **11.1** Watch part of Erik Johansson's TED Talk. Answer the questions with a partner.

1 Describe the image the speaker shows.

2 Johansson asks, "Is it photography?" What do you think? Is it?

11A Snapshots

Photographer Erik Johansson creates striking images that seem impossible.

VOCABULARY Photography

A Add the words to the word map.

camera	landscape	background	picture	shape	beautiful	weird

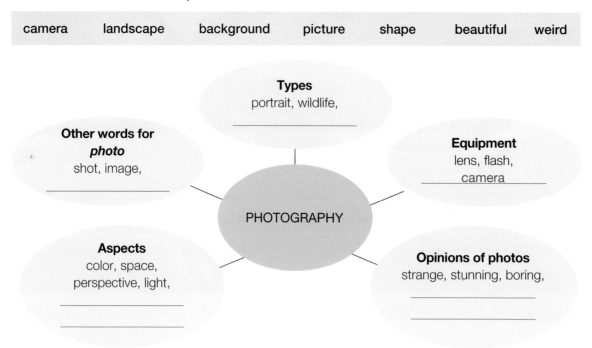

Types
portrait, wildlife,
_____

Other words for *photo*
shot, image,
_____

Equipment
lens, flash,
camera
_____

Aspects
color, space,
perspective, light,
_____
_____

PHOTOGRAPHY

Opinions of photos
strange, stunning, boring,
_____
_____

B Work with a partner. Look at the photo on this page. Describe the photo and say what you like about it.

It's a bit strange, but I really like it.

Me too. I love the background.

LISTENING My perfect photo

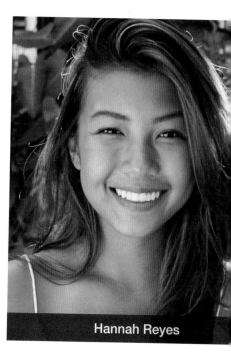

Hannah Reyes

> **Listening for opinions**
> When you listen for a speaker's opinion, listen for verbs like *think, believe, feel, seems,* and for expressions like *to me* and *in my opinion.*

A ▶ **11.2** Hannah Reyes is a travel photographer from the Philippines. Watch and check the things she says are important when taking a photo.

☐ using the right equipment

☐ being in the right place

☐ understanding light

B ▶ **11.2** Watch again. What's her favorite photo? Why does she like it?

C **CRITICAL THINKING**

Personalizing What things do you consider when taking a photo? Discuss with a partner.

SPEAKING Giving your opinion

A ▶ **11.3** A man and a woman are talking about the photo on page 120. Which person likes it more?

A: Hey, look at this picture.   image / photo

B: Wow! That's pretty cool.

A: It's really unusual, isn't it?   strange / weird

B: Yeah.

A: I love the colors and the use of space.   background / perspective

B: Yeah. But I think anyone can make a picture like this with a computer.

A: I don't think so. I think you still need real talent.   In my opinion, / To me,

B: I know what you mean. But I find real photos more interesting.

B Practice the conversation with a partner. Practice again using the words on the right.

C Work with a group. Find a photo you like on your phone. Describe the photo and say what you like about it. Use the words on page 120.

> I like this photo. I took it a few weeks ago in the park. I like the colors and the light.

> Yeah, it's beautiful.

11B What's your opinion?

LANGUAGE FOCUS Discussing opinions

A ▶ **11.4** Look at the image on the opposite page and read the information below.
Do you think the image is real or digitally altered? Discuss with a partner.

HOW TO TELL IF A PHOTO IS **NOT REAL**

Modern technology makes it possible to create and change images very easily. How can you tell if a photo is not real? Ask yourself these four questions.

Are there any differences in the lighting and shadows?

Is anything in the photo too big or too small?

Are there any strangely curved or bending surfaces?

Use your common sense— is anything else unusual?

B ▶ **11.5** Listen to two people discussing the image on the opposite page. Why do they think the image is not real?

C ▶ **11.6** Watch and study the language in the chart.

Asking for and giving opinions		
Do you think this photo is interesting?	Yes, I do. I think it's very interesting. No, I don't. I don't think it's interesting.	
What do you think of this image? How do you feel about this picture? What's your opinion of this shot?	I	think (that) it's amazing. feel (that) it's overrated. believe (that) it's her best one. find it boring.
	It	looks like a painting. looks fake.
	To me, it's kind of weird. In my opinion, it's stunning.	

For more information on **sense verbs**, see Grammar Summary 11 on page 158.

D Complete the questions and answers using the words in parentheses.

1 A: (how / feel / this picture) _____ ?

   B: (think / gorgeous) _____ .

2 A: (what / think / this landscape) _____ ?

   B: (find / a little boring) _____ .

3 A: (what / opinion / this portrait) _____ ?

   B: (not / believe / real) _____ .

4 A: (do / this picture / weird) _____ ?

   B: (yes / seems / strange) _____ .

E ▶ **11.7** Complete the information. Circle the correct words. Listen and check your answers.

Look at the picture on the right of what ¹(**looks** / **looks like**) a giant sink. What ²(**are you** / **do you**) think? Is it real or digitally altered?

At first glance, the image ³(**looks** / **looks like**) quite realistic. But take a closer look at the shadows and lighting, and you'll probably ⁴(**feel** / **look**) that something is not quite right.

With today's technology, it's not difficult to create a photo like this one and make people believe ⁵(**that** / **like**) it's real. This image was made by combining two simple photos—one of a young boy and one of a bathroom sink. The sink ⁶(**looks** / **looks like**) huge when compared to the size of the boy.

F Write your opinions. Then compare with a partner.

1 What do you think of the picture on page 88? _____ .

2 How do you feel about the photo on page 98? _____ .

3 What's your opinion of the photo on page 110? _____ .

SPEAKING Is it real?

A Turn to page 147 and look at the two photos. One is digitally altered, and one is real. Use the tips on page 122 to figure out which one is real.

B Discuss your ideas with a partner. Do you both agree?

> I think this one is real and this one is digitally altered.

> Why do you think so? It looks real to me.

Photo of camel thorn
trees by Frans Lanting

11C Unreal images of nature

PRE-READING Predicting

A Look at the title and the two photos. What do you think the text is mainly about?

a two photo contest winners   **b** famous fake photos   **c** amazing photos of nature

B Read the first paragraph. Check your prediction.

▶ 11.8

1 These days, even an **amateur** photographer—armed only with a smartphone—can take a simple picture and transform it into a thing of beauty. The photos here, however, are a 5 reminder that perhaps the most amazing images are not those **enhanced** by computer software, but created by nature itself.

Photo of camel thorn trees by Frans Lanting

Frans Lanting **captured** this stunning landscape 10 image of camel thorn trees in a location called Dead Vlei in Namibia. Due to the nature of the lighting in the frame, the photograph looks like a painting.

In the photo, the trees appear against a bright background. The background appears to be an 15 orange-colored sky, but it is in fact a sand dune[1] dotted with white grasses. Lanting got the shot at **dawn** when the light of the morning sun lit up the dune. The ground looks blue because it's reflecting the color of the sky above.

20 ### Photo of camel shadows by Chris Johns

Chris Johns shot this photo (page 125) of a group of camels crossing the desert near Lake Assal in Djibouti, one of the lowest points on Earth.

The camels appear dark against the light-colored 25 sand. However, what the viewer sees as a camel is actually its **shadow**. The camels are the thin brown lines. Johns took the photo from straight above the animals. The late afternoon sun casts the long shadows.

[1] **dune:** *n.* a large hill of sand formed by the wind

124

UNDERSTANDING MAIN IDEAS

Check [✓] the statements that the author of the article would most likely agree with.

☐ Modern technology makes it easy for people to create a beautiful photo.

☐ Computer-produced images are now more amazing than real photographs.

☐ The photos mentioned in the article show that you don't need a computer to create amazing images.

UNDERSTANDING DETAILS

A Complete the Venn diagram using the information below.

a taken in Africa

b taken in the morning

c taken in the afternoon

d taken from above

e uses sand as a background

f taken from the ground

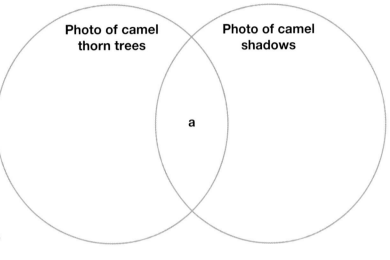

Photo of camel thorn trees

Photo of camel shadows

a

B Circle the correct option to complete the sentences below.

a When Lanting took the photo, the sky was (**orange** / **blue**).

b The thin brown lines in Chris Johns's photo are (**camels** / **shadows**).

BUILDING VOCABULARY

A Choose the correct words.

1 If you **enhance** something, you make it (**better** / **worse**).

2 If you are an **amateur**, you (**get paid** / **don't get paid**) for what you do.

3 You can **capture** an image with a (**camera** / **book**).

4 **Dawn** is in the (**morning** / **evening**).

5 You make a **shadow** by blocking (**sound** / **light**).

B **CRITICAL THINKING**

Applying Which photo from the reading do you think was more difficult to capture? Why? Discuss with a partner.

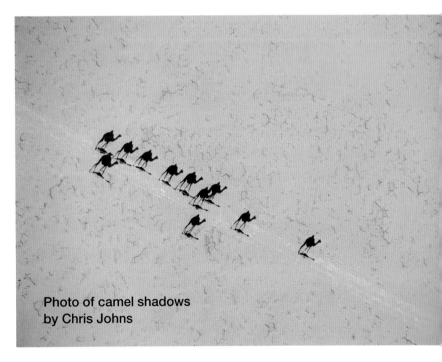

Photo of camel shadows by Chris Johns

11D Impossible photography

TEDTALKS

Erik Johansson loves to **combine** photos to create a **realistic**-looking image—but one that is often a kind of **illusion**. His idea worth spreading is that photography can be a highly creative medium that **tricks** the eye and captures an idea, rather than an actual moment or place.

PREVIEWING

Read the paragraph above. Match each **bold** word to its meaning. You will hear these words in the TED Talk.

1 not fake looking: _____

2 something that seems real but isn't: _____

3 deceive or fool: _____

4 join into one: _____

VIEWING

A ▶ **11.9** Watch Part 1 of the TED Talk. Circle the correct option to complete each sentence.

1 Johansson's passion for photography mixed with his earlier interest in (**drawing** / **computers**).

2 Johansson says that in regular photographs the process (**starts** / **ends**) when you take the photo.

3 In Johansson's images, most of the work is done (**before** / **after**) he takes the photo.

B ▶ **11.10** Watch Part 2 of the TED Talk. Complete the notes.

To create a combined realistic photo:

1 The two photos should have the same _____.

2 The two photos should have the same type of _____.

3 The two photos should be seamless so you can't see where one _____ and the other _____.

C ▶ **11.11** Watch Part 3 of the TED Talk. Check [✓] the statements that Johansson would agree with.

☐ It's important to plan very carefully to achieve a realistic result.

☐ You should sketch your idea before you take any photos.

☐ Today's technology is not yet good enough to create realistic looking images.

D CRITICAL THINKING

Evaluating In the talk, Johansson says, "It felt like photography was more about being at the right place at the right time. I felt like anyone could do that." Do you agree? Discuss with a partner.

VOCABULARY IN CONTEXT

▶ **11.12** Watch the excerpts from the TED Talk. Choose the correct meaning of the words.

PRESENTATION SKILLS Introducing a visual

Speakers often show visuals—photos, maps, charts, videos—to support their talks. Here are some ways to introduce a visual.

Here's a (picture/video) of …	*This is a (chart/map) of …*
In this …	*I want to share with you …*
I'd like to show you …	*Take a look at …*

A ▶ **11.13** Watch the excerpt of Johansson introducing a visual. Complete the sentences.

"I'm here to ¹_____ my photography. Or is it photography? Because, of course, ²_____ is a ³_____ that you can't take with your camera."

B ▶ **11.14** Now watch other TED speakers introduce visuals. Check [✓] the expressions you hear.

1 ☐ This is … **3** ☐ Here's … **5** ☐ In this …

2 ☐ Have a look. **4** ☐ I want to show you … **6** ☐ Let's have a look at …

C Work in a group. Show the other members of your group a photo or video from your phone. Say what it is.

" The result can be quite beautiful. "

11E Combining photos

COMMUNICATE Animal hybrids

A Work with a partner. Look at this photo of a "snowl leopard." The image combines two different animal photos. What do you think the two animals are?

B What two animals do you think are combined for these hybrid animals? What do you think each one looks like?

orangupanda	crocobear	butterphant	owloala

C Choose two animals to combine. Draw a sketch of it, give it an interesting name, and explain what's interesting about it.

> We could combine an octopus and a horse. We can call it an octohorse.

> Great idea! It can have the body of a horse and eight tentacles like an octopus.

Asking about spelling

How do you spell that?
Is that spelled with a d or a p?

D-E-N-G-U-I-N.
It's spelled with a d, as in dog.

D Go online and find possible photos to use that can combine well. Look back at Viewing Part B on page 126 to review Johansson's three rules for combining photos.

WRITING Describing a photo

Search online, or in this book, for a photo that you really like. Write a description of it. Explain what the photo shows and what you like about it.

> I really like the photo on page 41. It shows a surfer in the freezing cold. I love the lighting and the perspective. Just looking at the photo makes me feel cold.

12 Healthy Habits

6,600,000

TED

Myriam Sidibe
Public health expert, TED speaker

" Handwashing with soap is one of the most cost-effective ways of saving children's lives. **"**

UNIT GOALS

In this unit, you will …

- talk about health and good hygiene practices.
- read about the importance of handwashing.
- watch a TED Talk about a simple solution for preventing disease.

WARM UP

▶ **12.1** Watch part of Myriam Sidibe's TED Talk. Answer the questions with a partner.

1 How do you think the audience feels?

2 Read the quote from Sidibe above. How do you think handwashing with soap can save children's lives?

Thousands of people doing yoga at Red Rocks Park, Colorado

12A Staying healthy

VOCABULARY Habits

A Match the words in each set.

1 wash ○	○ breakfast
2 go ○	○ your hands
3 skip ○	○ to the gym
4 eat ○	○ snacks
5 brush ○	○ mouthwash
6 use ○	○ your teeth

7 avoid ○	○ vitamins
8 get ○	○ red meat
9 take ○	○ eight hours of sleep
10 do ○	○ a bike
11 ride ○	○ sugar-free soda
12 drink ○	○ yoga

B In your opinion, are the things in **A** good for your health, bad for your health, or do they make no difference? Complete the chart. Then compare your opinions with a partner.

Healthy	Makes no difference	Unhealthy

C Work with a partner. Share what you do to stay healthy.

I go to the gym and drink sugar-free soda.

I go to the gym, too. But I think sugar-free soda is unhealthy. I try to drink water instead.

LISTENING My healthy (and unhealthy) habits

> **Recognizing linking sounds**
> When we speak, we don't usually say – each – word – separately.
> Instead, we join, or link, words together. If you can recognize
> linking, it will increase your comprehension.
>
> take a vitamin   eight hours of sleep   have unhealthy habits

A ▶ **12.2** Watch David Matijasevich talking about some
of his habits. What does he say he does too much?

B ▶ **12.2** Watch again. Complete the notes.

David Matijasevich

Matijasevich's unhealthy habits	Matijasevich's healthy habits
• He drinks _____ cups of coffee a day. • He doesn't _____ enough.	• He never _____. • He takes _____. • He exercises. For example, he _____ and plays _____.

C CRITICAL THINKING

Evaluating Which of Matijasevich's habits do you think is the healthiest?
Discuss with a partner.

SPEAKING Talking about healthy options

A ▶ **12.3** Why doesn't speaker B drink sugar-free soda?

A: Do you want a soda?

B: Just water, thanks. I don't drink soda anymore.

A: Really? Why not?   How come? / What's the reason?

B: I saw a TV show about it last month.
When you drink a can of soda, you consume   If / Every time
eight teaspoons of sugar.

A: Wow! Well, I have some sugar-free soda.

B: Oh, someone told me that's even worse. I don't   apparently / I heard
think sugar substitutes are good for your health.   very healthy / good for you

A: OK, but I only have tap water. Is that okay?

B: You know, I'm not that thirsty actually.

B Practice the conversation with a partner. Practice again using the words on the right.

C Work with a partner. What kind of food or drink do you avoid? Explain your reasons.

> I try to avoid eating fast food. It's really unhealthy.

> Yeah, me too. I also avoid drinking too much coffee.

12B Healthy choices

LANGUAGE FOCUS Discussing hygiene

A ▶ **12.4** Read the information. What's the best method for drying your hands? Why?

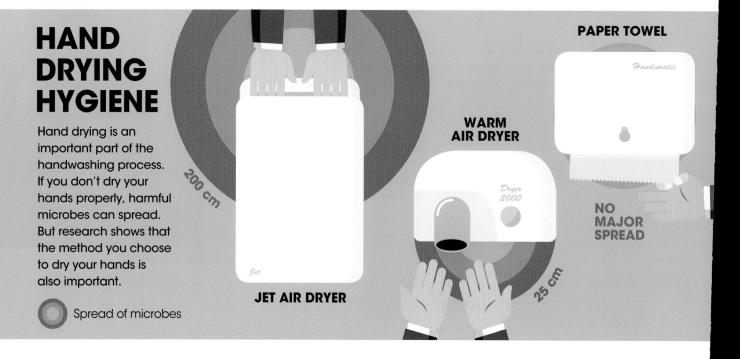

HAND DRYING HYGIENE

Hand drying is an important part of the handwashing process. If you don't dry your hands properly, harmful microbes can spread. But research shows that the method you choose to dry your hands is also important.

● Spread of microbes

JET AIR DRYER
WARM AIR DRYER
PAPER TOWEL

200 cm
25 cm

NO MAJOR SPREAD

B ▶ **12.5** Listen to an expert discuss hand drying. Complete the sentences.

1 After the expert washes her hands, she always uses _____ .

2 If you don't dry your hands at all, _____ .

C ▶ **12.6** Watch and study the language in the chart.

Talking about real conditions
If / When you drink a can of soda, you consume eight teaspoons of sugar. You consume eight teaspoons of sugar if / when you drink a can of soda.
What happens if / when you dry your hands with a warm-air dryer? If / When you dry your hands with a warm-air dryer, what happens?

When Whenever Every time	I dry my hands, I use a paper towel.

For more information on **real conditionals**, see Grammar Summary 12 on page 158.

D Write the words and phrases in the correct order to make sentences.

1 it relaxes / take a hot bath / When / it / your whole body / you

_____

2 a healthy breakfast / eat / If / energy for the day / it gives you / you

_____

3 get stronger / lift weights regularly / if / Your muscles / you

_____

E ▶ **12.7** Complete the information using the correct form of the words. Listen and check your answers.

Hand sanitizers are everywhere these days, but are they a good thing?

In short, yes, but be careful. Any hand sanitizer should contain at least 60 percent alcohol. If it ¹_____ (contain) less, it ²_____ (not kill) harmful bacteria.

Hand sanitizers are certainly convenient, but they should not replace regular handwashing. For example, if your hands ³_____ (be) very dirty, it ⁴_____ (be) much better to wash them with soap and water.

Also, be careful not to use hand sanitizers too often. When you ⁵_____ (overuse) sanitizer, the alcohol ⁶_____ (dry) out your skin.

SPEAKING Healthy choices

A Read the sentences below. Do you think these are healthy choices? Discuss with a partner. Explain your answers.

"If I need a late night snack, I eat something low in sugar."

"When I'm feeling stressed, I play computer games."

"If I feel like I'm getting a cold, I go to bed early and rest."

"If there's no hand towel in the bathroom, I dry my hands on my jeans."

"When I'm feeling tired in the evening, I drink coffee."

B Work with another partner. Find out what he or she does in the situations described above.

What do you do if you need a late night snack?

I try not to eat anything. If I'm really hungry, I eat something light.

Kenyan schoolchildren wash their hands during Global Handwashing Day.

12C A simple solution

PRE-READING Skimming

Skim the passage and look at the lesson title, photo, and captions. What is it mainly about?

a the work of a public health expert in Africa

b why people take part in Global Handwashing Day

▶ **12.8**

1 Each October 15, over 200 million people around the world take part in **Global Handwashing Day**. But why dedicate a day to something we do all the time? Well, research shows that not enough people regularly wash their hands with soap. Experts believe that this leads to the deaths of millions of people every year.

2 Myriam Sidibe says that soap is "the most beautiful invention in public health." As a public health expert, Sidibe knows that washing your hands with soap can have a huge impact on reducing flu,[1] cholera,[2] and the **spread** of other diseases. It can reduce diarrhea[3] by half and respiratory infections[4] by one-third. Handwashing with soap **prevents** babies from getting sick and keeps children healthy and in school.

3 However, washing hands with soap does not occur as **frequently** as you might think. This is partly due to a lack of resources in poorer countries, but it's also because for many people, handwashing is simply not part of their everyday routine. It's not easy to get people to change habits they've had since early childhood—but this is what Global Handwashing Day aims to do.

4 In 2008, the Indian cricket team joined around 100 million Indian schoolchildren in washing their hands to promote the first ever Global Handwashing Day. Every year since then, the campaign has held many different events around the world. In 2014, Global Handwashing Day was used in the fight against Ebola, with events held in affected African countries.

5 Today, local and national leaders continue to use the day to spread the message about the value of clean hands. The hope is that handwashing can become a regular part of people's lives and make a **vital** difference to the health of millions around the world.

[1] **flu:** *n.* (short for **influenza**) a common illness that causes fever, weakness, and body aches

[2] **cholera:** *n.* a serious disease of the small intestine

[3] **diarrhea:** *n.* an illness that causes you to pass waste from your body frequently

[4] **respiratory infection:** a disease that affects your breathing

IDENTIFYING PURPOSE

Read the passage. Match each paragraph to its purpose.

1 Paragraph 1 ○   ○ suggests why many people don't wash their hands.

2 Paragraph 2 ○   ○ describes what Global Handwashing Day hopes to achieve.

3 Paragraph 3 ○   ○ describes the benefits of handwashing with soap.

4 Paragraph 4 ○   ○ gives examples of Global Handwashing Day events.

5 Paragraph 5 ○   ○ introduces Global Handwashing Day.

UNDERSTANDING DETAILS

Answer the questions. Check all answers that apply.

1 Which aims of Global Handwashing Day are mentioned in the passage?

☐ to teach people about the importance of handwashing

☐ to make people use less water when they wash their hands

☐ to make handwashing part of everyone's routine

2 Which benefits of handwashing with soap are mentioned in the passage?

☐ Children miss fewer days of school because they're healthier.

☐ It prevents us from catching diseases from animals.

☐ It stops us spreading diseases to babies.

3 According to the passage, what is challenging about getting people to wash their hands?

☐ Habits are hard to change.

☐ People often ignore advice about health.

☐ People don't trust their governments.

Global Handwashing Day aims to make handwashing part of everyone's routine.

BUILDING VOCABULARY

A Match the words in **blue** from the passage to their definitions.

1 **global**   ○   ○ absolutely necessary

2 **prevent** ○   ○ involving the whole world

3 **vital**   ○   ○ to keep something from happening

B Choose the correct option to complete each sentence.

1 The **spread** of a disease refers to the disease _____.

a decreasing   b increasing

2 If something happens **frequently**, it happens _____.

a often   b rarely

C CRITICAL THINKING

Applying What other things can people do to help prevent the spread of diseases? Discuss with a partner.

12D The simple power of handwashing

TEDTALKS

MYRIAM SIDIBE is a public health expert. She feels we don't always need new technological **innovations** to prevent the spread of diseases. Her idea worth spreading is that the **availability** of soap and the habit of handwashing can greatly reduce disease and child **mortality** around the world.

PREVIEWING

Read the paragraph above. Circle the correct meaning of each **bold** word. You will hear these words in the TED Talk.

1 An **innovation** is a (**new** / **traditional**) idea or method.

2 The **availability** of something refers to how easy it is to (**find** / **use**).

3 **Mortality** refers to the (**birth** / **death**) of people or animals.

VIEWING

A ▶ **12.9** Watch Part 1 of the TED Talk. Answer the questions.

1 Look at the slide from Sidibe's TED Talk. What does it represent?

a the amount of money we can save by washing our hands

b the number of children who die before their fifth birthday every day

> **60 JUMBO JETS**

2 According to Sidibe, handwashing with soap can save how many children every year?

B ▶ **12.10** Watch Part 2 of the TED Talk. Complete the summary with words from the box. Four words are extra.

available	diseases	five	free	laundry
mortality	wash	ten	TVs	waste

Around the world, four out of ¹_____ people don't wash their hands after they use the toilet. This is true for countries where child ²_____ is high. But it's also true in richer countries that have soap, running water, and fancy toilets. In some poorer countries, it's because soap is used for ³_____ and washing dishes. Soap is ⁴_____, but it's precious, so a family may keep it in a cupboard so that people don't ⁵_____ it. However, this causes children at home to pick up ⁶_____ more easily.

C ▶ **12.11** Watch Part 3 of the TED Talk. Answer the questions.

1 How many people has Sidibe's handwashing program reached?

    a around 8 million   **b** around 100 million   **c** around 200 million

2 How many people does Sidibe's team hope to reach by 2020?

    a around 500 million   **b** around one billion   **c** around 5 billion

D CRITICAL THINKING

Interpreting Why do you think Sidibe told the story of the mother from Myanmar? Discuss with a partner.

VOCABULARY IN CONTEXT

▶ **12.12** Watch the excerpts from the TED Talk. Choose the correct meaning of the words.

PRESENTATION SKILLS Getting the audience's attention

> It's important to get the audience's attention at the start of a presentation. For example, you can:
>
> Tell a personal story.   Give an interesting quote.   Show a photo or video.
>
> Ask an interesting question.   Give a surprising fact or statistic.

A ▶ **12.13** Watch the excerpt. How does Sidibe get the audience's attention?

    a She tells a story.   **b** She gives a quote.   **c** She gives a statistic.

B ▶ **12.14** Do you remember how these TED speakers get their audience's attention? Match the speaker to the technique he or she uses. Then watch and check.

1 Meaghan Ramsey ○   ○ uses a video.

2 Chris Burkard ○   ○ gives a statistic.

3 Yves Rossy ○   ○ shows a photo and asks a question.

C Work in a group. Imagine you are going to give a presentation on the correct way to brush your teeth. How would you get your audience's attention?

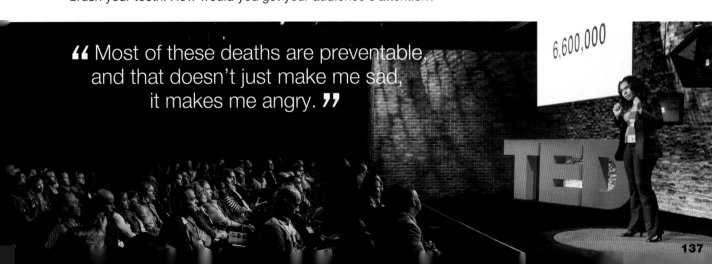

“ Most of these deaths are preventable, and that doesn't just make me sad, it makes me angry. ”

6,600,000

12E Food hygiene

COMMUNICATE Fact or myth?

A Work with a partner. Read the sentences about food hygiene below. Decide if each one is a fact or a myth. Explain your answers.

1 You should always throw food away after the "best before" date.
Fact   Myth

2 If you drop food on the floor, it's safe to eat if you pick it up quickly.
Fact   Myth

3 A wooden cutting board is more hygienic than a plastic one.
Fact   Myth

4 You need to wash raw chicken before you cook it.
Fact   Myth

5 A beef steak is safe to eat if only the outside is brown.
Fact   Myth

6 A hamburger is safe to eat if only the outside is brown.
Fact   Myth

7 It's important to keep uncooked food below cooked food in your fridge.
Fact   Myth

> I think number one is definitely a myth.

> Really? Why do you think so?

B Turn to page 147 and read the answers. Was anything surprising? Discuss with your partner.

> **Disagreeing politely**
> *I don't really agree.*   *Sorry, but I have to disagree.*
> *Actually, I have a different idea.*   *I'm not quite sure about that.*

WRITING Health tips

Imagine it's flu season. Think of and write the three tips for avoiding its spread.

> The most important thing to do is not share food or drinks. If you share food or drinks, you spread your germs. Another tip is to always cover your mouth when you cough or sneeze ...

Presentation 4

MODEL PRESENTATION

A Complete the transcript of the presentation using the words in the box.

| background | believe | heavy | if | maybe | opinion |
| picture | safe | second | should | space | take |

Let me tell you about my neighborhood—it's a place called Wallingden. Here you can see that it's quite a beautiful place. There is a lot of green ¹_____, and it's a really nice place to live. But it has a problem. ²_____ a look at this photograph. This is a ³_____ of Market Street in the morning. You can see that the traffic is really ⁴_____. Now, in the ⁵_____ of the image you can see a school bus. The road is right outside our local school. ⁶_____ children walk to school in the morning, they have no ⁷_____ place to cross this road. In my ⁸_____, this is really dangerous.

I ⁹_____ there are two things the local government needs to do. First, they ¹⁰_____ build a pedestrian crossing near the school, so children can cross safely. ¹¹_____, they need to do something to reduce the traffic to stop so many cars using this road. ¹²_____ they can build another road nearby.

But there's also something we can do. We need to write a letter to the local government to tell them about the problem. I really hope that they listen.

Thank you so much.

B ▶ P.4 Watch the presentation and check your answers.

C ▶ P.4 Review the list of presentation skills from Units 1–12 below. Which does the speaker use? Check [✓] each skill used as you watch again.

The speaker …
- introduces himself ☐
- gets the audience's attention ☐
- uses effective body language ☐
- introduces his topic ☐
- uses effective hand gestures ☐
- involves the audience ☐

- gives some statistics ☐
- shows enthusiasm ☐
- pauses effectively ☐
- paraphrases key points ☐
- uses visuals ☐
- thanks the audience ☐

YOUR TURN

A You are going to plan and give a short presentation to a partner about a problem in your neighborhood, city, or country. Use some or all the questions below to make some notes.

> What place are you going to talk about?
>
> What exactly is the problem?
>
> How can the problem be solved in your opinion?
>
> What steps need to be taken?

B Look at the useful phrases in the box below. Think about which ones you will need in your presentation.

> **Useful phrases**
>
> **Qualities of a neighborhood:** *clean streets, affordable housing, heavy traffic, reliable public transportation, friendly neighbors, high crime, good nightlife, green space*
>
> **Giving opinions:** *I think / believe / feel that … / To me, … / In my opinion, …*
>
> **Making Suggestions:** *We should … / Maybe we can … / One thing we could do is …*
>
> **Describing steps:** *Firstly, … / Secondly, … / Thirdly, …*

C Work with a partner. Take turns giving your presentation using your notes. Use some of the presentation skills from Units 1–12. As you listen, check [✓] each skill your partner uses.

The speaker …

• introduces himself / herself	☐	• gives some statistics	☐
• gets the audience's attention	☐	• shows enthusiasm	☐
• uses effective body language	☐	• pauses effectively	☐
• introduces his or her topic	☐	• paraphrases key points	☐
• uses effective hand gestures	☐	• uses visuals	☐
• involves the audience	☐	• thanks the audience	☐

D Give your partner some feedback on their talk. Include two things you liked, and one thing he or she can improve.

> That was great. You paused effectively, and you used great visuals. But you didn't look at the audience enough.

Communication Activities

3E COMMUNICATE

STUDENT A

A The sentences below describe one of the jobs on page 42. Read the sentences to your partner. After each sentence, your partner can have one guess about what the job is. Your partner will score points depending on how quickly he or she can guess.

1 I usually work inside. (5 points for a correct guess after this sentence)

2 I don't usually work long hours. (4 points)

3 I often work alone. (3 points)

4 I need to be creative. (2 points)

5 I often use a guitar or piano. (1 point)   **(Answer – Songwriter)**

B Now listen to your partner's sentences. Try to guess the job.

9B SPEAKING

STUDENT B

You and Student A have the same story. Read the story and write questions to ask for the missing information. Then take turns asking questions to complete the story.

2 How _____ in the South Pacific?

4 How many times _____?

6 Where _____?

8 What _____?

She traveled across the South Pacific. Conditions there were not so dangerous. There were few storms, and she spent her time [2]_____.

She then sailed across the Atlantic Ocean around South America. The Atlantic Ocean was very dangerous. During one storm, her boat rolled over [4]_____ times.

The halfway point of her journey was on January 25, 2010. It was her 100th day at sea. Jessica continued on her journey, through the Indian Ocean and across southern Australia.

On May 15, 2010, she arrived [6]_____ after a journey of 210 days. Thousands of fans greeted her. How did she feel at the end? "I wanted to keep going," she wrote on her blog. She received [8]_____ for her achievement. She was named Young Australian of the Year in 2011.

6B SPEAKING

STUDENT A

These are exercises you can do before or during an exam to help reduce stress. Look at the pictures and read the text. Then cover the text and explain to Student B how to do each one.

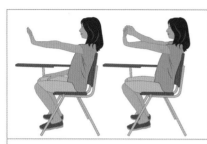 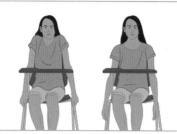 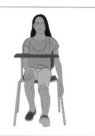 

Wrist exercises	Shoulder exercises	Leg and feet exercises
Straighten your left arm and point your fingers up. Then, with your right hand, pull back on your left-hand fingers gently, and hold. Repeat with other hand.	First, lift both of your shoulders slowly to your ears. Don't move, and hold. After three seconds, relax your shoulders. Repeat five times.	Before you begin, turn slightly in your chair. Stretch your left leg out. Then move your foot in circles. Do this for 15 seconds. Then repeat with right leg.

This exercise is for your wrists. First, straighten your left arm and point your fingers up.

Like this?

8B SPEAKING

STUDENT B

Read each question and the three choices to your partner. Mark each guess. Then see how many questions your partner got correct. (Correct answers are in **bold**.)

1 Death Valley is the lowest point in which country?

   a Egypt   **b** China   **c the United States**

2 The Gobi Desert covers almost 1.3 million square kilometers. Which one of these deserts is smaller?

   a the Sahara   **b the Atacama**   **c** the Arabian

3 They are called seas, but they're really lakes. Which is the largest?

   a the Caspian Sea   **b** the Aral Sea   **c** the Dead Sea

4 The deepest spot on Earth is in which ocean?

   a the Atlantic   **b** the Indian   **c the Pacific**

5 What is the biggest island in the world?

   a Madagascar   **b Greenland**   **c** New Guinea

1 Are you good with animals?

Yes, she is good with ani

2 Are you good at math?

No

3 Are you good at talking to people?

NO

4 Can you write well?

NO

5 Can you make people laugh easily?

NO

6 Are you interested in fashion?

No

7 Are you good at swimming?

Yes

8 Are you good at giving presentations?

NO

9 Can you sing and/or dance?

NO

10 Are you good at making things?

Yes

11 Are you good at taking photos?

yes

12 Are you good at giving advice?

Yes

13 Can you play a musical instrument?

Yes

14 Are you good at cooking?

Yes

15 Do you know how to speak a foreign language?

Yes

NO

JOB VACANCIES		
Birthday party clown Dress up like a clown and entertain at kids' parties.	**Wedding planner** Plan weddings for busy couples.	**Theme park character** Dress up like a cartoon character or celebrity.
Swimming pool lifeguard Keep swimmers safe at a local public swimming pool.	**Math teacher** Teach math at a local school.	**Underwater photographer** Take photos of underwater animals.
Museum tour guide Guide visitors and give presentations.	**Dolphin trainer** Help train dolphins to perform shows.	**Vacation cooking teacher** Teach foreign visitors how to cook local food.
Food blogger Review and write about today's coolest restaurants.	**Celebrity clothes buyer** Search for and buy clothes for your celebrity boss.	**Pet store assistant** Help care for animals, and take money from customers.
Video game designer Create and program new video games.	**Tourist office assistant** Answer questions and help tourists.	**Cruise ship entertainer** Sing and dance to entertain passengers.

3E COMMUNICATE

STUDENT B

A Your partner will read 5 sentences that describe one of the jobs on page 42. After each sentence, you can have one guess about what the job is. You will score points depending on how quickly you can guess.

B The sentences below describe one of the jobs on page 42. Read the sentences to your partner. After each sentence, your partner can have one guess about what the job is. Your partner will score points depending on how quickly he or she can guess.

1 I sometimes work long hours. (5 points for a correct guess after this sentence)

2 I work as part of a team. (4 points)

3 I sometimes work inside, and sometimes outside. (3 points)

4 A lot of people would like my job. (2 points)

5 Many people eat popcorn when they watch me. (1 point)

(Answer – Movie Actor)

thousand

9B SPEAKING

STUDENT A

You and Student B have the same story. Read the story and write questions to ask for the missing information. Then take turns asking questions to complete the story.

1 Where *did she travel* ?

3 What *was the atlantic ocean book* like?

5 When *was the halfway point of her journey*

7 Who *is greeted her ?* ?

She traveled across ¹ *the south Pacific* . Conditions there were not so dangerous. There were few storms, and she spent her time reading and doing her schoolwork.

She then sailed across the Atlantic Ocean around South America. The Atlantic Ocean was very ³ *dangerous* . During one storm, her boat rolled over four times.

The halfway point of her journey was ⁵ *On January 25th 2010* . It was her 100th day at sea. Jessica continued on her journey, through the Indian Ocean and across southern Australia.

On May 15, 2010, she arrived in Sydney Harbour after a journey of 210 days. ⁷ *thousan of fan* greeted her. How did she feel at the end? "I wanted to keep going," she wrote on her blog. She received a medal for her achievement. She was named Young Australian of the Year in 2011.

6B SPEAKING

STUDENT B

These are exercises you can do before or during an exam to help reduce stress. Look at the pictures and read the text. Then cover the text and explain to Student A how to do each one.

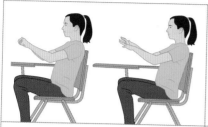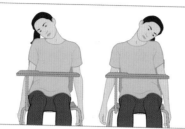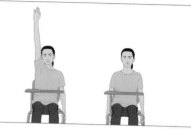

Hand exercises
First, make a tight ball with both hands. Hold for two seconds. Next, open your hands quickly and stretch your fingers out. Repeat eight times.

Neck exercises
Touch your right ear to your right shoulder. Hold for five seconds. Then touch your left ear to your left shoulder. Hold for five seconds. Repeat five times.

Arm exercises
Raise your right arm. When you cannot lift it any higher, relax and bring your arm down. Lift it again, trying to reach as high as you can. Do five times. Then repeat with left arm.

> This exercise is for your hands. First, make a tight ball with your hands.

> Like this?

8B SPEAKING

STUDENT A

Read each question and the three choices to your partner. Mark each guess. Then see how many questions your partner got correct. (Correct answers are in **bold**.)

1 Where is the world's highest mountain outside Asia?
   a **Argentina**   b Switzerland   c Kenya

2 What is the world's largest archipelago—or group of islands?
   a Canary Islands   b French Polynesia   c **Indonesia**

3 Which one of these islands is bigger than Iceland?
   a Bali   b Easter Island   c **Cuba**

4 Which U.S. state is the farthest south?
   a Florida   b **Hawaii**   c Texas

5 Which of these is the largest?
   a **the Indian Ocean**   b the Mediterranean Sea   c the Arctic Ocean

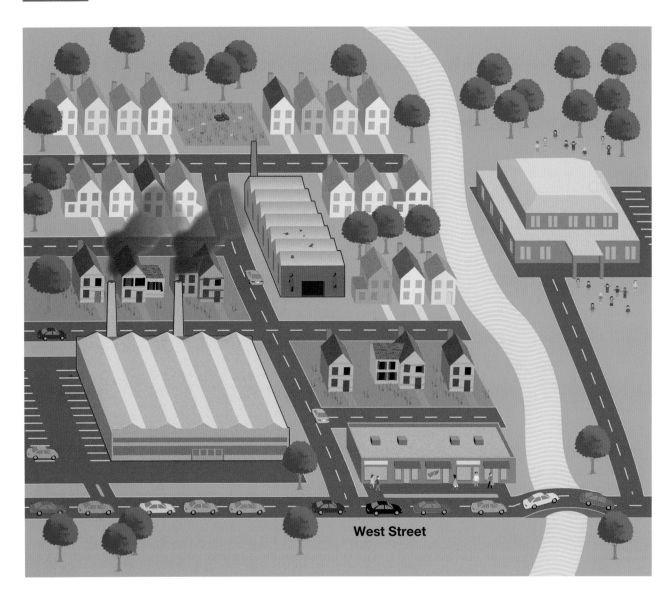

West Street

Read the problems below and find them on the neighborhood map.

- There are no parks downtown.
- There are a lot of vacant buildings.
- The traffic on West Street is very heavy.
- It takes a long time for children to get to school from their homes.
- The air quality is poor.
- There is very little entertainment.
- There aren't enough stores.
- There is no public transportation.

12E COMMUNICATE

Food hygiene: Fact or myth?

1 **Myth.** "Best before" dates are used to show when the food is best to eat. Most food is still safe to eat after the "best before" date. However, don't eat food after the "use by" date!

2 **Myth.** As soon as food touches the floor, it will pick up germs.

3 **Myth.** There's no difference between wooden and plastic cutting boards. Whichever you use, it needs to be clean.

4 **Myth.** Germs are easily spread by the water as you wash the chicken. Cooking the chicken properly will get rid of any germs.

5 **Fact.** Any germs will be on the outside of a steak. So if you cook the outside it's safe to eat.

6 **Myth.** Most burgers are made from chopped meat. This means that germs could be on the inside. It's important to cook the middle of any burger.

7 **Fact.** This is to stop bacteria from uncooked food dripping down onto cooked food.

Source: www.food.gov.uk

TED Talk Transcripts

Unit 1 Sleepy Man Banjo Boys: Bluegrass from New Jersey

Robbie Mizzone: Thank you.

Tommy Mizzone: Thank you very much. We're so excited to be here. It's such an honor for us. Like he said, we're three brothers from New Jersey—you know, the bluegrass capital of the world. We discovered bluegrass a few years ago, and we fell in love with it. We hope you guys will, too.

RM: I'm just going to take a second to introduce the band. On guitar is my 15-year-old brother Tommy. On banjo is 10-year-old Jonny. He's also our brother. And I'm Robbie, and I'm 14, and I play the fiddle.

[. . .] I'm also going to explain, a lot of people want to know where we got the name Sleepy Man Banjo Boys from. So it started when Jonny was little, and he first started the banjo, he would play on his back with his eyes closed, and we'd say it looked like he was sleeping.

[Music]

TM: Thank you very much.

RM: Thank you.

Unit 2 Jessi Arrington: Wearing nothing new

Part 1

I'm Jessi, and this is my suitcase. But before I show you what I've got inside, I'm going to make a very public confession, and that is, I'm outfit-obsessed. I love finding, wearing—and more recently—photographing, and blogging a different, colorful, crazy outfit for every single occasion. But I don't buy anything new. I get all my clothes secondhand from flea markets and thrift stores. Aww, thank you. Secondhand shopping allows me to reduce the impact my wardrobe has on the environment and on my wallet. I get to meet all kinds of great people; my dollars usually go to a good cause; I look pretty unique; and it makes shopping like my own personal treasure hunt. I mean, what am I going to find today? Is it going to be my size? Will I like the color? Will it be under $20? If all the answers are "yes," I feel as though I've won.

Part 2

And I'd really love to show you my week's worth of outfits right now. Does that sound good?

So as I do this, I'm also going to tell you a few of the life lessons that, believe it or not, I have picked up in these adventures wearing nothing new. So let's start with Sunday. I call this "Shiny Tiger." You do not have to spend a lot of money to look great. You can almost always look phenomenal for under $50.

[. . .] Monday: Color is powerful. It is almost physiologically impossible to be in a bad mood when you're wearing bright red pants. [Laughter] If you are happy, you are going to attract other happy people to you.

Tuesday: Fitting in is way overrated. I've spent a whole lot of my life trying to be myself and at the same time fit in. Just be who you are.

[. . .] Wednesday: Embrace your inner child. Sometimes people tell me that I look like I'm playing dress-up, or that I remind them of their seven-year-old. I like to smile and say, "Thank you."

Thursday: Confidence is key. If you think you look good in something, you almost certainly do. And if you don't think you look good in something, you're also probably right.

[. . .] Friday: A universal truth—five words for you: Gold sequins go with everything.

And finally, Saturday: Developing your own unique personal style is a really great way to tell the world something about you without having to say a word. It's been proven to me time and time again as people have walked up to me this week simply because of what I'm wearing, and we've had great conversations.

So obviously this is not all going to fit back in my tiny suitcase. So before I go home to Brooklyn, I'm going to donate everything back. Because the lesson I'm trying to learn myself this week is that it's OK to let go. I don't need to get emotionally attached to these things because around the corner, there is always going to be another crazy, colorful, shiny outfit just waiting for me, if I put a little love in my heart and look.

Thank you very much. Thank you.

Unit 3 Chris Burkard: The joy of surfing in ice-cold water

Part 1

So if I told you that this was the face of pure joy, would you call me crazy? I wouldn't blame you, because every time I look at this Arctic selfie, I shiver just a little bit. I want to tell you a little bit about this photograph.

I was swimming around in the Lofoten Islands in Norway, just inside the Arctic Circle, and the water was hovering right at freezing.

[. . .] Now, before we get into the why would anyone ever want to surf in freezing cold water, I would love to give you a little perspective on what a day in my life can look like.

[Video] Man: I mean, I know we were hoping for good waves, but I don't think anybody thought that was going to happen. I can't stop shaking. I am so cold.

Part 2

So, surf photographer, right? I don't even know if it's a real job title, to be honest. My parents definitely didn't think so when I told them at 19 I was quitting my job to pursue this dream career: blue skies, warm tropical beaches, and a tan that lasts all year long. I mean, to me, this was it. Life could not get any better. Sweating it out, shooting surfers in these exotic tourist destinations. But there was just this one problem. You see, the more time I spent traveling to these exotic locations, the less gratifying it seemed to be. I set out seeking adventure, and what I was finding was only routine.

[. . .] There's only about a third of the Earth's oceans that are warm, and it's really just that thin band around the equator. So if I was going to find perfect waves, it was probably going to happen somewhere cold, where the seas are notoriously rough, and that's exactly where I began to look. And it was my first trip to Iceland that I felt like I found exactly what I was looking for.

I was blown away by the natural beauty of the landscape, but most importantly, I couldn't believe we were finding perfect waves in such a remote and rugged part of the world.

[. . .] And I realized, all this shivering had actually taught me something: In life, there are no shortcuts to joy. Anything that is worth pursuing is going to require us to suffer just a little bit, and that tiny bit of suffering that I did for my photography, it added a value to my work that was so much more meaningful to me than just trying to fill the pages of magazines.

[. . .] So I look back at this photograph. It's easy to see frozen fingers and cold wet suits and even the struggle that it took just to get there, but most of all, what I see is just joy.

Thank you so much.

Unit 4 Tom Thum: The orchestra in my mouth

Part 1

We're going to take it back, way back, back into time. [Beatboxing: "Billie Jean"]

[Applause] All right. Wassup. Thank you very much, TEDx.

If you guys haven't figured it out already, my name's Tom Thum, and I'm a beatboxer, which means all the sounds that you just heard were made entirely using just my voice, and the only thing was my voice. And I can assure you there are absolutely no effects on this microphone whatsoever.

And I'm very, very stoked—you guys are just applauding for everything. It's great. Look at this, Mom! I made it!

[. . .] You know, I'm from Brisbane, which is a great city to live in. Yeah! All right! Most of Brisbane's here. That's good. You know, I'm from Brissy, which is a great city to live in, but let's be honest—it's not exactly the cultural hub of the Southern Hemisphere. So I do a lot of my work outside Brisbane and outside Australia, and so the pursuit of this crazy passion of mine has enabled me to see so many amazing places in the world.

Part 2

I would like to share with you some technology that I brought all the way from the thriving metropolis of Brisbane. These things in front of me here are called Kaoss Pads, and they allow me to do a whole lot of different things with my voice. For example, the one on the left here allows me to add a little bit of reverb to my sound, which gives me that— [Trumpet]—flavor. [Laughter] And the other ones here, I can

use them in unison to mimic the effect of a drum machine or something like that. I can sample in my own sounds and I can play it back just by hitting the pads here. [Applause]

I got way too much time on my hands. And last but not least, the one on my right here allows me to loop loop loop loop loop loop loop loop my voice.

Part 3

So with all that in mind, ladies and gentlemen, I would like to take you on a journey to a completely separate part of Earth as I transform the Sydney Opera House into a smoky downtown jazz bar. All right boys, take it away. [Music]

Ladies and gentlemen, I'd like to introduce you to a very special friend of mine, one of the greatest double bassists I know. Mr. Smokey Jefferson, let's take it for a walk. Come on, baby. [Music]

All right, ladies and gentlemen, I'd like to introduce you to the star of the show, one of the greatest jazz legends of our time. Music lovers and jazz lovers alike, please give a warm hand of applause for the one and only Mr. Peeping Tom. Take it away. [Music] [Applause]

Thank you. Thank you very much.

Unit 5 Yves Rossy: Fly with the Jetman

Part 1

Narrator: Many of the tests are conducted while Yves is strapped onto the wing, because Yves' body is an integral part of the aircraft. The wing has no steering controls, no flaps, no rudder. Yves uses his body to steer the wing. When he arches his back, he gains altitude. When he pushes his shoulders forward, he goes into a dive.

[. . .] Commentator One: There he goes. There is Yves Rossy. And I think the wing is open. So our first critical moment, it's open. He is down. Is he flying?

Commentator Two: It looks like he's stabilized. He's starting to make his climb.

Commentator One: There's that 90 degree turn you're talking about, taking him out over the channel. There is Yves Rossy. There is no turning back now. He is over the English Channel and under way. Ladies and gentlemen, a historic flight has begun.

[. . .] Commentator One: There he is. Yves Rossy has landed in England.

Bruno Giussani: And now he's in Edinburgh. Yves Rossy! [Applause]

Part 2

[What's it like up there?]

Yves Rossy: It's fun. It's fun. I don't have feathers. But I feel like a bird sometimes. It's really an unreal feeling, because normally you have a big thing, a plane, around you. And when I strap just this little harness, this little wing, I really have the feeling of being a bird.

[How did you become Jetman?]

It was about 20 years ago, when I discovered free falling. When you go out of an airplane, you are almost naked. You take a position like that. And especially when you take a tracking position, you have the feeling that you are flying. And that's the nearest thing to the dream. You have no machine around you. You are just in the element. It's very short and only in one direction.

[What's your top speed?]

It's about 300 kilometers per hour before looping. That means about 190 miles per hour.

[What's the weight of your equipment?]

When I exit full of kerosene, I'm about 55 kilos. I have 55 kilos on my back.

[What's next for Jetman?]

YR: First, to instruct a younger guy. I want to share it, to do formation flights. And I plan to start from a cliff, like catapulted from a cliff.

BG: So instead of jumping off a plane, yes?

YR: Yes, with the final goal to take off, but with initial speed. Really, I go step by step. It seems a little bit crazy, but it's not. It's possible to start already now, it's just too dangerous. Thanks to the increasing technology, better technology, it will be safe. And I hope it will be for everybody.

BG: Yves, thank you very much. Yves Rossy.

Unit 6 Daniel Kish: How I use sonar to navigate the world

Part 1

[Clicking]

[. . .] Many of you may have heard me clicking as I came onto the stage—[Clicking]—with my tongue. Those are flashes of sound that go out and reflect from surfaces all around me, just like a bat's sonar, and return to me with patterns, with pieces of information, much as light does for you. And my brain, thanks to my parents, has been activated to form images in my visual cortex, which we now call the imaging system, from those patterns of information, much as your brain does. I call this process flash sonar. It is how I have learned to see through my blindness, to navigate my journey through the dark unknowns of my own challenges . . .

Part 2

[. . .] But I was not raised to think of myself as in any way remarkable. I have always regarded myself much like anyone else who navigates the dark unknowns of their own challenges. Is that so remarkable? I do not use my eyes; I use my brain. Now, someone, somewhere, must think that's remarkable, or I wouldn't be up here, but let's consider this for a moment.

Everyone out there who faces or who has ever faced a challenge, raise your hands. Whoosh. OK. Lots of hands going up, a moment, let me do a head count. This will take a while. OK, lots of hands in the air. Keep them up. I have an idea. Those of you who use your brains to navigate these challenges, put your hands down. OK, anyone with your hands still up has challenges of your own.

Part 3

[. . .] So now I present to you a challenge. So if you'd all close your eyes for just a moment, OK? And you're going to learn a bit of flash sonar. I'm going to make a sound. I'm going to hold this panel in front of me, but I'm not going to move it. Just listen to the sound for a moment. Shhhhhhhhhh. OK, nothing very interesting. Now, listen to what happens to that same exact sound when I move the panel. Shhhhhhhhhh.

[. . .] OK, now keep your eyes closed because, did you hear the difference? OK. Now, let's be sure. For your challenge, you tell me, just say "now" when you hear the panel start to move. OK? We'll relax into this. Shhhhhhhhhh.

Audience: Now.

Daniel Kish: Good. Excellent. Open your eyes. All right. So just a few centimeters, you would notice the difference. You've experienced sonar. You'd all make great blind people.

Part 4

Let's have a look at what can happen when this activation process is given some time and attention.

[Video] Juan Ruiz: It's like you guys can see with your eyes, and we can see with our ears.

Brian Bushway: It's not a matter of enjoying it more or less, it's about enjoying it differently.

Shawn Marsolais: It goes across.

DK: Yeah.

SM: And then it's gradually coming back down again.

DK: Yes!

SM: That's amazing. I can, like, see the car. Holy mother!

J. Louchart: I love being blind. If I had the opportunity, honestly, I wouldn't go back to being sighted.

JR: The bigger the goal, the more obstacles you'll face, and on the other side of that goal is victory. [In Italian]

DK: Now, do these people look terrified? Not so much. We have delivered activation training to tens of thousands of blind and sighted people from all backgrounds in nearly 40 countries. When blind people learn to see, sighted people seem inspired to want to learn to see their way better, more clearly, with less fear, because this exemplifies the immense capacity within us all to navigate any type of challenge, through any form of darkness, to discoveries unimagined when we are activated. I wish you all a most activating journey.

Thank you very much.

Unit 7 Meaghan Ramsey: Why thinking you're ugly is bad for you

Part 1

When is it suddenly not OK to love the way that we look? Because apparently we don't. Ten thousand people every month google, "Am I ugly?"

This is Faye. Faye is 13, and she lives in Denver. And like any teenager, she just wants to be liked and to fit in. It's Sunday night. She's getting ready for the week ahead at school. And she's slightly dreading it, and she's a bit confused because despite her mom telling her all the time that she's beautiful, every day at school, someone tells her that she's ugly. Because of the difference between what her mom tells her and what her friends at school, or her peers at school, are telling her, she doesn't know who to believe. So, she takes a video of herself. She posts it to YouTube and she asks people to please leave a comment: "Am I pretty or am I ugly?"

[. . .] Thousands of people are posting videos like this, mostly teenage girls, reaching out in this way. But what's leading them to do this? Well, today's teenagers are rarely alone. They're under pressure to be online and available at all times, talking, messaging, liking, commenting, sharing, posting—it never ends.

[. . .] This always-on environment is training our kids to value themselves based on the number of likes they get and the types of comments that they receive. There's no separation between online and offline life. What's real or what isn't is really hard to tell the difference between.

Part 2

Surely we want our kids to grow up as healthy, well-balanced individuals. But in an image-obsessed culture, we are training our kids to spend more time and mental effort on their appearance at the expense of all of the other aspects of their identities. So, things like their relationships, the development of their physical abilities, and their studies, and so on, begin to suffer. Six out of ten girls are now choosing not to do something because they don't think they look good enough.

[. . .] Thirty-one percent, nearly one in three teenagers, are withdrawing from classroom debate. They're failing to engage in classroom debate because they don't want to draw attention to the way that they look. One in five are not showing up to class at all on days when they don't feel good about it. And when it comes to exams, if you don't think you look good enough, specifically if you don't think you are thin enough, you will score a lower grade point average than your peers who are not concerned with this. And this is consistent across Finland, the U.S., and China, and is true regardless of how much you actually weigh. So to be super clear, we're talking about the way you think you look, not how you actually look.

Part 3

We need to start judging people by what they do, not what they look like. We can all start by taking responsibility for the types of pictures and comments that we post on our own social networks. We can compliment people based on their effort and their actions and not on their appearance.

[. . .] Ultimately, we need to work together as communities, as governments, and as businesses to really change this culture of ours so that our kids grow up valuing their whole selves, valuing individuality, diversity, inclusion. We need to put the people that are making a real difference on our pedestals, making a difference in the real world.

[. . .] Right now, our culture's obsession with image is holding us all back. But let's show our kids the truth. Let's show them that the way you look is just one part of your identity and that the truth is we love them for who they are and what they do and how they make us feel. Let's build self-esteem into our school curriculums. Let's each and every one of us change the way we talk and compare ourselves to other people. And let's work together as communities, from grassroots to governments, so that the happy little one-year-olds of today become the confident changemakers of tomorrow. Let's do this.

Unit 8 Karen Bass: Unseen footage, untamed nature

Part 1

As a filmmaker, I've been from one end of the Earth to the other trying to get the perfect shot and to capture animal behavior never seen before. And what's more, I'm really lucky, because I get to share that with millions of people worldwide. Now the idea of having new perspectives of our planet and actually being able to get that message out gets me out of bed every day with a spring in my step.

You might think that it's quite hard to find new stories and new subjects, but new technology is changing the way we can film. It's enabling us to get fresh, new images and tell brand new stories.

[. . .] For a filmmaker, new technology is an amazing tool, but the other thing that really, really excites me is when new species are discovered. Now, when I heard about one animal, I knew we had to get it for my next series, *Untamed Americas,* for National Geographic.

Part 2

In 2005, a new species of bat was discovered in the cloud forests of Ecuador. And what was amazing about that discovery is that it also solved the mystery of what pollinated a unique flower. It depends solely on the bat.

[Video] Narrator: The tube-lipped nectar bat. A pool of delicious nectar lies at the bottom of each flower's long flute. But how to reach it? Necessity is the mother of evolution. [Music] This two-and-a-half-inch bat has a three-and-a-half-inch tongue, the longest relative to body length of any mammal in the world. If human, he'd have a nine-foot tongue.

KB: What a tongue! We filmed it by cutting a tiny little hole in the base of the flower and using a camera that could slow the action by 40 times. So imagine how quick that thing is in real life.

Part 3

Now people often ask me, "Where's your favorite place on the planet?" And the truth is I just don't have one. There are so many wonderful places. But some locations draw you back time and time again. And one remote location—I first went there as a backpacker; I've been back several times for filming, most recently for *Untamed Americas*—it's the Altiplano in the high Andes of South America, and it's the most otherworldly place I know. But at 15,000 feet, it's tough. It's freezing cold, and that thin air really gets you. Sometimes it's hard to breathe, especially carrying all the heavy filming equipment.

[. . .] But the advantage of that wonderful thin atmosphere is that it enables you to see the stars in the heavens with amazing clarity. Have a look.

[Video] Narrator: Some 1,500 miles south of the tropics, between Chile and Bolivia, the Andes completely change. It's called the Altiplano, or "high plains"—a place of extremes and extreme contrasts. Where deserts freeze and waters boil. More like Mars than Earth, it seems just as hostile to life. The stars themselves—at 12,000 feet, the dry, thin air makes for perfect stargazing. Some of the world's astronomers have telescopes nearby. But just looking up with the naked eye, you really don't need one.

KB: Thank you so much for letting me share some images of our magnificent, wonderful Earth. Thank you for letting me share that with you.

Unit 9 Robert Swan: Let's save the last pristine continent

Part 1

Let's go south. All of you are actually going south. This is the direction of south, this way, and if you go 8,000 kilometers out of the back of this room, you will come to as far south as you can go anywhere on Earth, the Pole itself.

Now, I am not an explorer. I'm not an environmentalist. I'm actually just a survivor, and these photographs that I'm showing you here are dangerous. They are the ice melt of the South and North Poles. And ladies and gentlemen, we need to listen to what these places are telling us, and if we don't, we will end up with our own survival situation here on planet Earth.

I have faced head-on these places, and to walk across a melting ocean of ice is without doubt the most frightening thing that's ever happened to me.

[. . .] In this photograph, we are standing in an area the size of the United States of America, and we're on our own. We have no radio communications, no backup. Beneath our feet, 90 percent of all the world's ice, 70 percent of all the world's freshwater. We're standing on it. This is the power of Antarctica.

On this journey, we faced the danger of crevasses, intense cold, so cold that sweat turns to ice inside your clothing, your teeth can crack, water can freeze in your eyes. Let's just say it's a bit chilly. [Laughter] And after 70 desperate days, we arrive at the South Pole. We had done it.

Part 2

For the last 11 years, we have taken over 1,000 people, people from industry and business, women and men from companies, students from all over the world, down to Antarctica, and during those missions, we've managed to pull out over 1,500 tons of twisted metal left in Antarctica. That took eight years, and I'm so proud of it because we recycled all of it back here in South America.

[. . .] We have taken young people from industry and business from India, from China. These are game-changing nations, and will be hugely important in the decision about the preservation of the Antarctic.

[. . .] It is such a privilege to go to Antarctica, I can't tell you. I feel so lucky, and I've been 35 times in my life, and all those people who come with us return home as great champions, not only for Antarctica, but for local issues back in their own nations.

Part 3

NASA informed us six months ago that the Western Antarctic Ice Shelf is now disintegrating. Huge areas of ice—look how big Antarctica is even compared to here—huge areas of ice are breaking off from Antarctica, the size of small nations. And NASA have calculated that the sea level will rise, it is definite, by 1 meter in the next 100 years, the same time that my mum has been on planet Earth. It's going to happen, and I've realized that the preservation of Antarctica and our survival here on Earth are linked. And there is a very simple solution. If we are using more renewable energy in the real world, if we are being more efficient with the energy here, running our energy mix in a cleaner way, there will be no financial reason to go and exploit Antarctica. It won't make financial sense, and if we manage our energy better, we also may be able to slow down, maybe even stop, this great ice melt that threatens us.

[. . .] Antarctica is a moral line in the snow, and on one side of that line we should fight, fight hard for this one beautiful, pristine place left alone on Earth. I know it's possible. We are going to do it. And I'll leave you with these words from Goethe. I've tried to live by them.

"If you can do, or dream you can, begin it now, for boldness has genius, power, and magic in it."

Good luck to you all. Thank you very much.

Unit 10 Theaster Gates: How to revive a neighborhood

Part 1

The neighborhood that I live in is Grand Crossing. It's a neighborhood that has seen better days. It is not a gated community by far. There is lots of abandonment in my neighborhood, and while I was kind of busy making pots and busy making art and having a good art career, there was all of this stuff that was happening just outside my studio.

[. . .] But I think a lot of our U.S. cities and beyond have the challenge of blight—abandoned buildings that people no longer know what to do anything with. And so I thought, is there a way that I could start to think about these buildings as an extension or an expansion of my artistic practice? And that if I was thinking along with other creatives—architects, engineers, real estate finance people—that us together might be able to kind of think in more complicated ways about the reshaping of cities.

Part 2

And so I bought a building. The building was really affordable. We tricked it out. We made it as beautiful as we could to try to just get some activity happening on my block. Once I bought the building for about $18,000, I didn't have any money left. So I started sweeping the building as a kind of performance. This is performance art, and people would come over, and I would start sweeping. Because the broom was free and sweeping was free. It worked out. [Laughter] But we would use the building, then, to stage exhibitions, small dinners, and we found that that building on my block, Dorchester—we now referred to the block as Dorchester Projects—that in a way that building became a kind of gathering site for lots of different kinds of activity.

[. . .] One house turned into a few houses, and we always tried to suggest that not only is creating a beautiful vessel important, but the contents of what happens in those buildings is also very important. So we were not only thinking about development, but we were thinking about the program, thinking about the kind of connections that could happen between one house and another, between one neighbor and another.

Part 3

In this bank that we called the Arts Bank, it was in pretty bad shape. There was about six feet of standing water. It was a difficult project to finance, because banks weren't interested in the neighborhood because people weren't interested in the neighborhood because nothing had happened there. It was dirt. It was nothing. It was nowhere. And so we just started imagining, what else could happen in this building?

And so now that the rumor of my block has spread, and lots of people are starting to visit, we've found that the bank can now be a center for exhibition, archives, music performance, and that there are people who are now interested in being adjacent to those buildings because we brought some heat, that we kind of made a fire.

[. . .] In some ways, it feels very much like I'm a potter, that we tackle the things that are at our wheel, we try with the skill that we have to think about this next bowl that I want to make. And it went from a bowl to a singular house to a block to a neighborhood to a cultural district to thinking about the city, and at every point, there were things that I didn't know that I had to learn.

[. . .] So now, we're starting to give advice around the country on how to start with what you got, how to start with the things that are in front of you, how to make something out of nothing, how to reshape your world at a wheel or at your block or at the scale of the city.

Thank you so much.

Unit 11 Erik Johansson: Impossible photography

Part 1

I'm here to share my photography. Or is it photography? Because, of course, this is a photograph that you can't take with your camera.

Yet, my interest in photography started as I got my first digital camera at the age of 15. It mixed with my earlier passion for drawing, but it was a bit different because using the camera, the process was in the planning instead. And when you take a photograph with a camera, the process ends when you press the trigger. So to me it felt like photography was more about being at the right place and the right time. I felt like anyone could do that.

So I wanted to create something different, something where the process starts when you press the trigger. Photos like this: construction going on along a busy road. But it has an unexpected twist. And despite that, it retains a level of realism. Or photos like these—both dark and colorful, but all with a common goal of retaining the level of realism.

Part 2

But what's the trick that makes it look realistic? Is it something about the details or the colors? Is it something about the light? What creates the illusion?

[. . .] I would like to say that there are three simple rules to follow to achieve a realistic result. As you can see, these images aren't really special. But combined, they can create something like this.

So the first rule is that photos combined should have the same perspective. Secondly, photos combined should have the same type of light. And these two images both fulfill these two requirements—shot at the same height and in the same type of light. The third one is about making it impossible to distinguish where the different images begin and end by making it seamless. Make it impossible to say how the image actually was composed.

Part 3

So to achieve a realistic result, I think it comes down to planning. It always starts with a sketch, an idea. Then it's about combining the different photographs. And here every piece is very well planned. And if you do a good job capturing the photos, the result can be quite beautiful and also quite realistic. So all the tools are out there, and the only thing that limits us is our imagination.

Thank you.

Unit 12 Myriam Sidibe: The simple power of handwashing

Part 1

So imagine that a plane is about to crash with 250 children and babies, and if you knew how to stop that, would you?

Now imagine that 60 planes full of babies under 5 crash every single day. That's the number of kids that never make it to their fifth birthday: 6.6 million children never make it to their fifth birthday.

Most of these deaths are preventable, and that doesn't just make me sad, it makes me angry, and it makes me determined. Diarrhea and pneumonia are among the top two killers of children under five, and what we can do to prevent these diseases isn't some smart new technological innovations. It's one of the world's oldest inventions: a bar of soap.

[. . .] Handwashing with soap is one of the most cost-effective ways of saving children's lives. It can save over 600,000 children every year. That's the equivalent of stopping ten jumbo jets full of babies and children from crashing every single day.

Part 2

So now just take a minute. I think you need to get to know the person next to you. Why don't you just shake their hands? Please shake their hands. All right, get to know each other. They look really pretty. All right. So what if I told you that the person whose hands you just shook actually didn't wash their hands when they were coming out of the toilet? They don't look so pretty anymore, right? Pretty yucky, you would agree with me.

Well, statistics are actually showing that four people out of five don't wash their hands when they come out of the toilet, globally. And the same way, we don't do it when we've got fancy toilets, running water, and soap available, it's the same thing in the countries where child mortality is really high.

[. . .] So why is it? Why aren't people washing their hands? Why is it that Mayank, this young boy that I met in India, isn't washing his hands? Well, in Mayank's family, soap is used for bathing, soap is used for laundry, soap is used for washing dishes. His parents think sometimes it's a precious commodity, so they'll keep it in a cupboard. They'll keep it away from him so he doesn't waste it. On average, in Mayank's family, they will use soap for washing hands once a day at the very best, and sometimes even once a week for washing hands with soap. What's the result of that? Children pick up disease in the place that's supposed to love them and protect them the most, in their homes.

Part 3

Nine years ago, I decided, with a successful public health career in the making, that I could make the biggest impact coming, selling, and promoting the world's best invention in public health: soap. We run today the world's largest handwashing program by any public health standards. We've reached over 183 million people in 16 countries. My team and I have the ambition to reach one billion by 2020.

[. . .] Last week, my team and I spent time visiting mothers that have all experienced the same thing: the death of a newborn. I'm a mom. I can't imagine anything more powerful and more painful. This one is from Myanmar. She had the most beautiful smile, the smile, I think, that life gives you when you've had a second chance. Her son, Myo, is her second one. She had a daughter who passed away at three weeks, and we know that the majority of children that actually die, die in the first month of their life, and we know that if we give a bar of soap to every skilled birth attendant, and that if soap is used before touching the babies, we can

reduce and make a change in terms of those numbers.

[. . .] I hope you will join us and make handwashing part of your daily lives and our daily lives and help more children like Myo reach their fifth birthday.

Thank you.

Grammar Summary

UNIT 1: Simple present

I love hip-hop. She loves pop. I don't like jazz. She doesn't like R&B. Do you like K-pop? 　　Yes, I do. / No, I don't. Does he like rap? 　　Yes, he does. / No, he doesn't.	We use the simple present to talk about … • our likes and dislikes. 　*I love hip-hop.* • our habits and routine. 　*I listen to music every day.* • things that are always true. 　*I come from Brazil.*

UNIT 2: Adverbs of frequency

I often buy used clothes. I sometimes shop online. I hardly ever buy video games. I never spend money on makeup. Do you ever shop online? Yes, I often do. / No, I rarely do. How often do you go to the mall? I go once a week.	• We use adverbs of frequency to say how often something happens. 　*I always pay for things with cash.* • The adverb goes before the main verb. 　*I usually buy things on sale.* • We can also use time expressions to express frequency. 　*I buy coffee every day.*

Time expressions

once twice three times	a	day week month year

once	every	few days two weeks six months four years

UNIT 3: *Be like, like,* and *would like*

What's your job like? It's really easy. What are your hours like? They're pretty long. What do you like about your job? I like the people. What job would you like to have someday? I'd love to be a TV presenter.	• When we want someone to describe something, we can ask, *What's … like?* 　*What's your job like? (It's really easy.)* • To ask what someone likes or enjoys, we can ask, *What do you like about …?* 　*What do you like about your new job?* • To ask what someone wants to do, we can ask, *What would you like to …?* 　*What job would you like to have someday?*

UNIT 4: *Can* and *can't*

I can sing. I can't dance.
She can dance. She can't sing.
 	
Can you speak Korean?
Yes, I can. / No, I can't.
 	
What languages can you speak?
I can speak Spanish and English.
	• We use *can* to talk about abilities.
	  I can sing. I can't dance.
	
	• The verb after *can* does not change.
	  I can drive. She can drive. They can drive.
	
	• The negative of *can* is *cannot*, or *can't*.
	  I cannot / can't speak Thai.

UNIT 5: Quantifiers

There are only a few songs on your phone.
There aren't many songs on your phone.
There aren't a lot of songs on your phone.
 	
There's only a little music on your phone.
There's not much music on your phone.
There isn't a lot of music on your phone.
 	
How many songs do you have? A lot.
 	
How much music do you have? A lot.
	• Quantifiers answer the questions *How many?* or *How much?*
	
	• Some are used for things we can count.
	  How many of your friends are online now?
	  There aren't many. There are a few.
	
	• Some are used for things we can't count.
	  How much time do we have?
	  We don't have much. We have only a little.
	
	• *A lot of* can be used for things we can count or things we can't.
	  I have a lot of videos / time.

Common uncountable nouns

advice	ice	love	music	rain
air	information	luck	nature	rice
fun	joy	luggage	news	traffic
furniture	litter	money	paper	trash

UNIT 6: Time clauses

Before I get home, I usually pick up some groceries.
 	
When I don't know a word in English, I look it up in a dictionary.
 	
After I answer all the exam questions, I look them over one more time.
	• Time clauses can be used at the start or end of a sentence.
	  When I have an exam, I get nervous.
	  I get nervous when I have an exam.
	
	• Remember to use a comma when the time clause is at the start of the sentence.

UNIT 7: Modifying adverbs

She's extremely hungry.
She's very / really happy.
She's pretty quiet.
She's fairly old.
She's somewhat talkative.
She's kind of / sort of unhappy.
She's a bit / a little heavy.
She's not hungry (at all).
 	
She's too hungry to wait.
	• *Extremely, very, really,* and *pretty* make an adjective stronger.
	  He's friendly. → *He's very friendly.*
	
	• *Fairly, somewhat, kind of, sort of,* and *a bit/ little* make the adjective less strong.
	  He's tired. → *He's kind of tired.*
	
	• *Too* means *more than necessary.*
	  She thinks she's too short.

UNIT 8: Comparative and superlative adjectives

Comparative adjectives Everest is higher than K-2. The Pacific is hotter than the Arctic. I think Hawaii is prettier than California. **Superlative adjectives** Russia is the biggest country in the world. Waikiki is the most famous beach in Hawaii. What do you think is the most beautiful city in Europe?	• For most one-syllable adjectives, add -er/-est: *small* → *smaller* → *smallest*. • For adjectives ending in y, change y to i and add -er/-est: *icy* → *icier* → *iciest*. • For some adjectives ending in a consonant, double it: *big* → *bigger* → *biggest*. • For some two- and all three-syllable adjectives, use more/the most: *famous > more famous > the most famous.*

UNIT 9: Simple past

He traveled to the Arctic.
He didn't travel to Antarctica.
 	
They flew in a balloon.
They didn't fly in a plane.
 	
Did she sail around the world?
Yes, she did. / No, she didn't.
 	
Where did they go?
They went to the moon.
	• We use the simple past to talk about completed actions in the past.
	  I worked late last night.
	  She went to Peru in 2014.
	
	• To form the simple past, for most verbs add -ed. For the negative, just add *didn't.*
	  He traveled by dogsled.
	  He didn't travel by plane.
	
	• There are many irregular past tense verbs. These need to be memorized.
	  come → *came, eat* → *ate, meet* → *met*

Common irregular verbs

bring	→ brought	drink	→ drank	know	→ knew	sing	→ sang
buy	→ bought	eat	→ ate	make	→ made	sleep	→ slept
catch	→ caught	find	→ found	meet	→ met	swim	→ swam
come	→ came	fly	→ flew	read	→ read	think	→ thought
cost	→ cost	get	→ got	see	→ saw	win	→ won
cut	→ cut	go	→ went	sell	→ sold	write	→ wrote

UNIT 10: *Should* and *shouldn't*

You should move to a new apartment.
You shouldn't stay in your current place.
 	
Should we live in the city center?
Yes, we should. / No, we shouldn't.
 	
What time should we leave for the airport?
We should leave at 4:15.
	We use *should* to:
	
	• say what is important for you to do.
	  I should go. I shouldn't stay.
	
	• give advice to others.
	  You should move. You shouldn't stay here.
	
	The verb after *should* does not change.
	I should go. You should go. They should go.

UNIT 11: Sense verbs

I feel tired.
You don't sound very good.
 	
Does this smell strange to you?
Yes, it does. / No, it doesn't.
 	
How does this taste?
It tastes great.
	• We often use verbs like *feel, sound, look, taste, smell,* and *seem* with adjectives, not adverbs.
	  This tastes too salty.
	  She seems a bit strange today.
	
	• We often use *How* to ask questions.
	  How does this hat look on me?

Questions with sense verbs

How does it	feel? sound? look? taste? smell?

What does it	feel sound look taste smell	like?

UNIT 12: Real conditionals

I can't sleep if/when I drink too much coffee.
If/When I drink too much coffee, I can't sleep.
 	
Do you skip your shower if/when there is no hot water?
 	
What do you do if/when you don't have any toothpaste?
	• You can use real conditionals with *if* or *when* to talk about:
	  • scientific facts.
	  If you heat water to 100°C, it boils.
	  • things that are always true.
	  When I wash my hands, I always use soap.
	
	• Both clauses are often in the simple present. If you begin with *If* or *When*, add a comma.
	  I wash with shampoo if I don't have soap.
	  If I don't have soap, I wash with shampoo.

Acknowledgements

The Author and Publisher would like to thank the following teaching professionals for their valuable input during the development of this series:

Coleeta Paradise Abdullah, Certified Training Center; **Tara Amelia Arntsen**, Northern State University; **Estela Campos**; **Federica Castro**, Pontificia Universidad Católica Madre y Maestra; **Amy Cook**, Bowling Green State University; **Carrie Cheng**, School of Continuing and Professional Studies, the University of Hong Kong; **Mei-ho Chiu**, Soochow University; **Anthony Sean D'Amico**, SDH Institute; **Wilder Yesid Escobar Almeciga**, Universidad El Bosque; **Rosa E. Vasquez Fernandez**, English for International Communication; **Touria Ghaffari**, The Beekman School; **Rosario Giraldez**, Alianza Cultural Uruguay Estados Unidos; **William Haselton**, NC State University; **Yu Huichun**, Macau University of Science and Technology; **Michelle Kim**, TOPIA Education; **Jay Klaphake**, Kyoto University of Foreign Studies; **Kazuteru Kuramoto**, Keio Senior High School; **Michael McCollister**, Feng Chia University; **Jennifer Meldrum**, EC English Language Centers; **Holly Milkowart**, Johnson County Community College; **Nicholas Millward**, Australian Centre for Education; **Stella Maris Palavecino**, Buenos Aires English House; **Youngsun Park**, YBM; **Adam Parmentier**, Mingdao High School; **Jennie Popp**, Universidad Andrés Bello; **Terri Rapoport**, ELS Educational Services; **Erich Rose**, Auburn University; **Yoko Sakurai**, Aichi University; **Mark D. Sheehan**, Hannan University; **DongJin Shin**, Hankuk University of Foreign Studies; **Shizuka Tabara**, Kobe University; **Jeffrey Taschner**, AUA Language Center; **Hadrien Tournier**, Berlitz Corporation; **Rosa Vasquez**, JFK Institute; **Jindarat De Vleeschauwer**, Chiang Mai University; **Tamami Wada**, Chubu University; **Colin Walker**, Myongii University; **Elizabeth Yoon**, Hanyang University; **Keiko Yoshida**, Konan University

And special thanks to: **Craig Albrightson, Sam Cossman and Matt Caltabiano, Ross Donihue and Marty Schnure, Stella Hekker, Philip Jones, Mary Kadera, Bonnie Kim, Scott Leefe, Richard Lenton, David Matijasevich, Hannah Reyes**

Credits

Photo Credits

Cover Diane Cook and Len Jenshel/National Geographic Creative, **3** Pablo Corral Vega/National Geographic Creative, **4** (tl) © James Duncan Davidson/TED, (tr) © Michael Brands/TED, (cl) © Bret Harman/TED, (cr) © TED, (bl) Christophe Vollmer/Reuters, (br) © Bret Hartman/TED, **5** (tl) © Ryan Lash/TED, (tr) © James Duncan Davidson/TED, (cl) © Ryan Lash/TED, (cr) © Bret Hartman/TED, (bl) © Erik Johansson, (br) © Ryan Lash/TED, **6** (tl1) © Glenn Oakley, (tl2) © Richard Nowitz/National Geographic Creative, (cl1) Robert Pratta/Reuters, (cl2) Essdras M Suarez/The Boston Globe/Getty Images, (bl1) Jbor/Shutterstock.com, (bl2) AP Images/The Commercial Appeal, Yalonda M. James, **8** (tl1) Ollyy/Shutterstock.com, (tl2) Pablo Corral Vega/National Geographic Creative, (cl1) Cory Richards/National Geographic Creative, (cl2) Eric Kruszewski/National Geographic Creative, (bl1) © Erik Johansson, (bl2) Blaine Harrington III/Getty Images, **10** © Bret Hartman/TED, **12** © Michael Brands/TED, **13** © James Duncan Davidson/TED, **14** © Glenn Oakley, **15** © Tony Gribben, **17** © William Thoren, **18** Joseph Llanes/Contour/Getty Images, **20** © Amy Harris, **21** © Michael Brands/TED, **22** MCarper/Shutterstock.com, **23** © Michael Brands/TED, **24** © Richard Nowitz/National Geographic, **25** © Stella Hekker, **27** Pedro Armestre/AFP/Getty Images, **28** © Atlantide Phototravel, **30** (tr) © Michael Brands/TED, (c) (bl) (br) © TED, **31** © TED, **32** BillionPhotos/Shutterstock.com, **33** © Bret Harman/TED, **34** Robert Pratta/Reuters, **35** © Richard Lenton, **37** Tiksa Negeri/Reuters, **38** Hiroyuki Ito/Hulton Archive/Getty Images, **40–41** © Chris Burkard/Massif, **42** Photobac/Shutterstock.com, **43** © Cengage Learning, **45** © TED, **46** Essdras M Suarez/The Boston Globe/Getty Images, **47** National Geographic Channel, **49** European Pressphoto Agency (EPA) b.v./Alamy Stock Photo, **50** Seong Joon Cho/Bloomberg/Getty Images, **52** © TED, **53** Guillem Lopez/Starstock/Photoshot/Newscom, **54** Jennifer Hayes/National Geographic Creative, **55** Christophe Vollmer/Reuters, **56** Jbor/Shutterstock.com, **57** Barcroft Media/Getty Images, **59** AP Images/PRNewsFoto/Arx Pax, **60** Wenn Ltd/Alamy Stock Photo, **62** (tr) © James Duncan Davidson/TED, (b) Unimedia Europe/Unimediaimages Inc/Unimedia Europe/Newscom, **63** Wenn Ltd/Alamy Stock Photo, **64** Christian Beutler/Keystone/Redux, **65** © Bret Hartman/TED, **66** AP Images/The Commercial Appeal, Yalonda M. James, **67** © Brian Mohr/EmberPhoto, **69** Cheryl Ravelo/Reuters, **70** Marco Grob/National Geographic Creative, **72** © Bret Hartman/TED, **73** ZUMA Press, Inc./Alamy Stock Photo, **74** Tom Wang/Shutterstock.com, **75** © Cengage Learning, **77** © Ryan Lash/TED, **78** Ollyy/Shutterstock.com, **79** © Bonnie Kim, **81** Purestock/Getty Images, **82** © Mark Henley/Panos, **84** © Ryan Lash/TED, **85** Phil McDonald/Shutterstock.com, **86** ©Malyugin/Shutterstock, **87** James Duncan Davidson/TED, **88** Pablo Corral Vega/National Geographic Creative, **89** © Rick Ridgeway, **91** Karen Kasmauski/National Geographic Creative, **92** Dordo Brnobic/National Geographic My Shot/National Geographic Creative, **94** James Duncan Davidson/TED, **95** Dordo Brnobic/National Geographic My Shot/National Geographic Creative, **96** Taylor Kennedy-Sitka Productions/National Geographic Creative, **97** © Ryan Lash/TED, **98** Cory Richards/National Geographic Creative, **99** © Scott Leefe, **101** © Erik Boomer, **102** © 2041foundation.org, **104** © Ryan Lash/TED, **105** Ralph Lee Hopkins/National Geographic Creative, **106** The Asahi Shimbun/Getty Images, **107** © Cengage Learning, **109** © Bret Hartman/TED, **110** Eric Kruszewski/National Geographic Creative, **111** (tr1) © Cengage Learning, (tr2) Africa Media Online/Alamy Stock Photo, **113** Christian Heeb/laif/Redux, **114** AP Images/Rex Features, **115** James S. Russell/Bloomberg/Getty Images, **116** © Bret Hartman/TED, **118** Richard Nowitz/National Geographic Creative, **119–120** © Erik Johansson, **121** Courtesy of Hannah Reyes, **122** (l1) © BoldStock/Unlisted Images, (l2) Vibrant Image Studio/Shutterstock.com, (cl) © ImageState, (cr) Creatas Images/Jupiterimages, (r) Comstock Images, **123** Thomas Jackson/Stone/Getty Images, **124** Frans Lanting/National Geographic Creative, **125** Chris Johns/National Geographic Creative, **126** © Robert Leslie/TED, **127** © Erik Johansson, **128** (tr1) Abeselom Zerit/Shutterstock.com, (tr2) FotoRequest/Shutterstock.com, (tr3) TTphoto/Shutterstock.com, **129** © Ryan Lash/TED, **130** Blaine Harrington III/Getty Images, **131** © Cengage Learning, **133** Yana Paskova/The New York Times/Redux, **134–135** Thomas Mukoya/Reuters, **136** © Ryan Lash/TED, **137** © Ryan Lash/TED, **138** Andrey Armyagov/Shutterstock.com, **139** © Cengage Learning, **147** (tl) Dean Lewins/EPA/Newscom, (tr1) Fabio Fersa/Shutterstock.com, (tr2) RTimages/Shutterstock.com, (tr3) Olena Dzekun/Shutterstock.com, (tr4) Elwynn/Shutterstock.com

Illustration & Infographic Credits

16, 26, 36, 48, 58, 68, 80, 90, 100, 112, 122, 132 emc design; **61, 71, 94, 117, 142, 145, 146** Ralph Voltz

Data sources for infographics: **16** Statista © 2016, **26** Piper Jaffray, **36** www.telegraph.co.uk, **80** GFK © 2015, **90** sevennaturalwonders.org, **112** CityLab © 2014, **132** www.europeantissue.com

Text Credits

70 Adapted from "Bat Man": ngm.nationalgeographic.com, June 2013